Cindy, Michelle, Traci
Purcell *Praise for W...*

I know from personal experience that abo... heart that can fester for a lifetime. Worthy of Love gives us a clear pathway ... healing and restoration as we offer up our wounds to the healing power of God's Word. Shadia's insights and Biblical teaching bring rich clarity to the forgiveness and love of Christ.

Theresa Ingram
Mentor, Speaker and Wife of Pastor and Author Chip Ingram

Engaging, intensely honest, vividly and poetically expressed, Shadia's story is sure to connect with the heart of its readers and draw them into their own journey of healing. Worthy of Love strikes an excellent balance of personal story-telling and solid biblical truth. Any woman seeking healing, freedom, and peace in the aftermath of an abortion will benefit greatly from this study.

S. Michael Houdmann, *President and Founder*
Got Questions Ministries

This book will minister to women and encourage them to not give in to despair as Shadia shows how the truth sets us free. One of the best post-abortion personal stories I've read and I've read a lot of them.

Georgette Forney
President of Anglicans for Life and Co-Founder of Silent No More

I was given an insider's peek into the healing journey of a deeply wounded heart transformed by the Master's touch. This book will breathe fresh hope and courage into every woman longing for a miracle of the heart.

Phyllis Bennett, *PhD*
Director Women's Center for Ministry, Western Seminary

From a desperate teenage choice, through shadowed valleys of shame and denial, Shadia's story packs more emotional energy than a dramatic novel and more wisdom than the world could hope to offer. This book should be read by anyone (including men) claiming to be pro-life as Shadia's story will inspire compassion and grace toward women deceived into making that fateful choice. For every woman who has carried a child and made the choice to abort, it is my prayer that they will discover the forgiveness and healing God desires to give.

Pastor David Nederhood, *Director of Ministry Relations*
KFAX Christian Radio, Salem San Francisco

Shadia bares her soul in this poignant yet uplifting story of incredible healing. You'll be moved to tears and to action by this important work. If more women would share their story, as Shadia has, then fewer women might walk the painful path. Shadia has captured, in a remarkable fashion, the beauty of redemption.

Austin Boyd
Award-winning Author and Speaker

What a beautiful work God is doing! This book is so Biblical and the processes you take each person through are so simple but profoundly effective. These steps mirror those our Heavenly Father took me through many years ago after sexual abuse (hidden 23 years!), three failed marriages, and a host of self imposed prison bars. Your work is a testimony to our Father's great love for us!

Becky Wood, *CEO*
ABC Women's Clinic of Dublin, GA

Shadia's story of her own painful experience is so powerful and the Biblical teaching is so healing. Like the title suggests, yes! you are 'worthy of love' and there is a healing at the end of the journey. I highly recommend it.

Matthew Lea, *PhD*
Licensed Marriage and Family Therapist, Professor, Pastor

A beautiful and heartfelt study for any woman who has suffered the shame and guilt of abortion. The Scriptures will ignite a woman's hope that she is forgiven and 'worthy of love.'

Jeannie Pittam, *Post Abortion Services Director*
Lincoln NE Crisis Pregnancy Center

Abortion breaks a woman's heart over and over but Worthy of Love open's up a door to healing, understanding, and forgiveness. Life changing and lovingly written.

Shellie Nichol
Host of Amazing Hope Radio and ordained Chaplain

I was very impressed with the breadth of Scripture and doctrinal soundness. I found the poetry refreshing and love its biblical basis. I highly recommend Worthy of Love.

Michele D. Shoun, *Director of Ministry Outreach*
Life Matters Worldwide

When I saw the title I immediately thought who wouldn't want to hear they are worthy of love? I love the gentleness of the language and especially enjoy the questions designed to help readers interact with Scripture. Thank you for giving us this great tool!

Carie White, *MA*
Licensed Professional Counselor

There's nothing more powerful than hearing someone's story and experiencing their pain and joy with them. I see God's heart in these Scriptures as it is He who heals us, and speaks to the broken places in our souls. The reflection questions are very effective in letting God draw out deep and hidden things of the heart. Love it!

Eileen Fahlgren, *Center Director*
Pregnancy Resource Centers of Central Oregon

I found your story to be powerful, important and very vulnerable. No wonder God has been using it to bring healing to so many. I praise God for what He has done in your life!

Kathy Collard Miller
Award Winning Author and Speaker

Worthy of Love

A JOURNEY OF HOPE AND HEALING AFTER ABORTION
with Biblical Reflections

Shadia Hrichi

"The degree to which you can tell your story
is the degree to which you can heal."

- Stasi Eldredge

LEADER'S GUIDE

Worthy of Love

A JOURNEY OF HOPE AND HEALING AFTER ABORTION
with Biblical Reflections

BEAUTIFUL VOICE MINISTRIES

Worthy of Love - Leader's Guide
Copyright © 2016 by Beautiful Voice Ministries and Shadia Hrichi

All rights reserved. No part of this book may be reproduced in whole or in part without written permission from the author, except by a reviewer who may include brief quotations in printed reviews; nor may any part of this book be reproduced, stored in a retrieval system, or transmitted in any form or by any means—electronic, mechanical, including photocopying, recording, or any other—without receiving prior permission in writing from the author, except as provided by USA copyright law.

Unless otherwise indicated, Scripture quotations are from the HOLY BIBLE, NEW INTERNATIONAL VERSION®, copyright © 1973, 1978, 1984 by International Bible Society. Used by permission of Zondervan Publishing House. All rights reserved.

Scripture quotations marked (NLT) are taken from the Holy Bible, New Living Translation, copyright © 1996, 2004. Used by permission of Tyndale House Publishers, Inc., Carol Stream, Illinois 60188. All rights reserved.

Scripture quotations marked (CEV) are taken from the Contemporary English Version Copyright © 1995 by American Bible Society. Used by permission.

Scripture quotations marked (ESV) are taken from The Holy Bible, English Standard Version® (ESV®). Copyright ©2001 by Crossway Bibles, a division of Good News Publishers. Used by permission. All rights reserved.

Scripture quotations marked (MSG) are taken from The Message. Copyright © 1993, 1994, 1995, 1996, 2000, 2001, 2002, 2003 by Eugene H. Peterson. Used by permission of NavPress Publishing Group.

Produced and published by
Beautiful Voice Ministries, San Jose, California
Edited in part by Judith Robl
Cover design by Lisa Hainline
Cover images: Dreamstime 10483527 © Y0jik, 23351633 © Macsim
Photograph on page 75: ©iStockphoto.com/Yuri
Persons depicted on cover and inteior are models and do not personally endorse
any business, product, service, cause, association or other endeavor.

ISBN 978-0-9897141-4-3

Printed in the United States of America

Acknowledgements

To my dear friend and ministry partner Sandi Miller: I am deeply indebted to you for your tireless support, prayers and love, which have carried me through many trials and triumphs over the past two years. Your compassionate dedication as a ministry partner and Worthy of Love Group Leader are a continuous source of blessing and encouragement not only to myself, but also to everyone God leads across your path as you serve Him. The invaluable feedback that you provided during the development of this Leader's Guide is greatly appreciated. I am truly humbled and filled with praise to God for His kindness in knitting our hearts together to serve Him in this tender work. Thank you, Sandi!

To Jeannie Pittam, Becky Wood, Sheryl Lynn Hoyle, Marcia Schillinger and so many others who serve alongside me in this ministry by leading Worthy of Love groups in your local pregnancy centers, churches, and homes. Thank you, dear sisters, for your partnership, prayers and encouragement. May our gracious Lord bless you as you minister to the women He entrusts to your care.

> "May the favor of the Lord our God rest on us;
> establish the work of our hands for us –
> yes, establish the work of our hands." (Psalm 90:17)

~

There are many people God has placed in my life for whom I am deeply grateful: my dear family, faithful friends including Leon and Erin Sivils, Carolyn Jacobsen, and Liz Nunez, God's servants at Western Seminary and Venture Christian Church, including the many wonderful pastors and professors who have taught and mentored me over the years. All of you have contributed in some special way to make me the person I am today. Because this book reaches into the very depths of my heart and soul, each one of you is a part of it as well.

I also wish to express my sincere appreciation to the following:

To Judith Robl, one of the primary cornerstones of this work. Your patient guidance and encouragement during my early years of writing are true gifts from the Lord. Your compassion for the unborn and women wounded by abortion, combined with your expert skills as an editor, have deeply enriched the narrative of this book. Being blessed by God with a powerful story and knowing how to share it effectively are two very different things; thank you for teaching me the power of storytelling.

To Dr. Phyllis Bennett, one of the first to affirm my calling as a Bible Teacher. Thank you for your valuable feedback and biblical insights as I prepared the reflection questions for each chapter. I am genuinely blessed by all of the ways you continue to cheer me on and support the work to which God has called me.

To Pastor Chip and Theresa Ingram. Thank you for all of the ways you courageously stand in defense of life while compassionately expressing God's love and grace to those wounded by abortion. Thank you especially for recommending this book. Together, you have stood by my side as pastor and mentor and faithful friends, sharing my joy with every step on the path God has laid before me.

To Brian Fisher, one of God's chief ambassadors for the unborn and all those wounded by abortion. Words cannot express how deeply humbled I am to partner with you in ministry. Your fearless pursuit of saving lives appears only matched by your compassion for those already wounded. I am truly honored for your willingness to write the Foreword to this book.

To all the saints at Venture Christian Church, my beloved brothers and sisters in Christ. For all that you do to minister to our Lord's family, serving one another in love, you have ministered to me. "As iron sharpens iron, so one person sharpens another." (Proverbs 27:17)

To all of God's servants at RealOptions, along with all those serving at countless other God-honoring pregnancy centers. May the Name of our Lord be lifted high for your courageous work and sacrificial love. Together, you serve as a beautiful model of the apostle Paul's exhortation, "Carry each other's burdens, and in this way you will fulfill the law of Christ." (Galatians 6:2)

Most of all, I am grateful to my glorious Lord and Savior Jesus Christ whose sacrificial love rescued my soul from death, my heart from grief and condemnation, and blessed my life beyond my wildest imagination. Your precious Word assures us, "There is therefore now no condemnation for those who are in Christ Jesus" (Romans 8:1). It is only by Your grace that I found the courage to share this story. By the power of Your Holy Spirit, I pray many hearts are healed for the glory of Your Kingdom.

And to every person reading this book: may you discover the magnificent love of Christ who longs to embrace you with the everlasting hope and healing each of our hearts is desperately searching for

– as these are found in no other Name.

In loving memory of

Amanda

Table of Contents

A Note from the Author

I once heard someone say, "There's a difference between forgiveness and healing," but it wasn't until God led me on a twenty-five year journey that I understood the profound truth of those words. This book is written from my heart to yours, as one who has been where you are.

Abortion is a deep and painful wound. Perhaps your wound is very recent, or maybe you're like me and buried the truth and memory of the abortion so deep and for so long, that you've almost forgotten about it. Almost. But God longs for us to be healed. In May 2008, God delivered my healing in the most miraculous way and I am honored to share with you my story. However, this study is more than one woman's journey; it is a reflection and reminder of God's tireless pursuit to draw us to Himself so that He can heal our deepest hurts and redeem our painful scars. Scars hidden so deep that, if left ignored, will forever hold us back from all that God desires for our lives.

God may have brought you to this study to introduce you to the grace of His forgiveness. Or it may be that you are here because God wants you to find the courage to forgive yourself . . . or someone else.

Even after embracing God's forgiveness, the wounds and aftermath of abortion can remain, perhaps for a lifetime, if we fail to address them. Wherever you are, God has brought you here for a purpose.

It is my prayer that through this study, God will bring you to a place where you will find both forgiveness and healing. We'll walk this road together, side by side. After you read a part of my journey, I encourage you to review the personal reflection section at the end of each chapter. The questions are designed for either group or individual study.

Remember dear Sister, while I journey with you in prayer, the Lord Himself will go with you. You are not alone:

"For I am the LORD your God who takes hold of your right hand and says to you, Do not fear; I will help you." -Isaiah 41:13

A special note for women who've experienced more than one abortion:
Although for the purpose of this study, abortion and children lost to abortion will often be referenced in the singular, if you've experienced more than one loss please know that you are not alone. As you answer the reflection questions, ask God to help you process each loss separately. If you need more space to write, you may wish to use a separate journal. God is our helper; He knows every detail of your situation and cares deeply for you. He is faithful and will be with you every step of the way.

What to expect: After reading a chapter, plan some time to complete the lesson, approximately one to two hours although it will be different for each person. The important thing is to take your time and allow God to speak to you. If He prompts you to meditate on something particular, give yourself permission to listen to God's voice, even if it means postponing finishing the lesson.

What you will need:
- A Bible or access to the Internet
- Pen/pencil
- A stack of blank 3x5 notecards
- Suggested: Journal

I am so excited for you! The hope that lies ahead will bring freedom to your heart in ways you never imagined possible. I'll see you on the other side.

Shadia

Foreword by Brian Fisher

The abuse of power and selfishness of my gender never ceases to grieve me. Our culture has come to believe that abortion is a "woman's" issue - that it is a private decision made only by women that has little or no consequence on themselves, the fathers, family members, or our communities.

Yet your hearts and tears tell a much different story.

Through our work at Online for Life, I've had the honor of getting to know women like you who have experienced abortion – whose pain, guilt, and grief are very real. Rather than experiencing the freedom of making a "reproductive choice," the decision to abort has lured many into an emotional and spiritual prison. I've listened to your stories about depression, shame, struggles with alcohol and substance abuse, and journeys to very dark and lonely places.

Many have told me, time and again, that if they had the ability to go back in time and take a different path, they would have chosen life for their children and, in turn, freedom for themselves.

But what grieves me the most is that many of you felt pressured, coerced even, by the father, family members, or friends, and that many of those voices belong to men and for that, I am exceedingly sorry.

I grieve also for men, for too many of us have abandoned our God-given roles as providers and protectors. Too many of us have succumbed to the lies of abortion. Too many of us sit by, whether actively or passively, and allow our children to lose their lives and their mothers to suffer immense pain.

But here's what I want you to know: not all of us are sitting by. More and more men are realizing the incalculable costs of abortion and they are running into the battle, determined to protect those in harm's way.

And yet, there is one Man who is greater than us all - who stepped into the battle knowing it would cost him his very life in order to offer us a life beyond imagination. There is one Man who so thoroughly honored, elevated, and encouraged women, that he was considered a revolutionary. He rescued them, protected them, restored them, redeemed them. And He forgave them.

And He still does so today.

The book you are holding is the result of that one Man and His profound, miraculous impact on one woman's life. That one Man, Jesus, broke into her abortion prison, restored her, refreshed her, and set her free.

Shadia's story, so powerfully and effectively shared, is a poignant, personal reminder that Jesus heals. He heals our broken hearts. He heals our crushed spirits. He heals our wounded souls.

And He wants to heal you.

You may be tempted to think that, because of the dramatic and miraculous way Jesus healed Shadia, His forgiveness can't possibly be for you. Abortion is just too great of a sin and you think you are beyond His mercy.

On the contrary, what Jesus provided for her, He will provide for you. He promises it.

I'm thrilled that Shadia took the time and effort to write this book. If more women and men were this honest and transparent about their abortion experience, we would see far less abortions in our country. I invite you to drink deep from her experience and her study of the Scriptures. Take your time, allow the words to work deep into your heart. Allow Jesus to lovingly, carefully, and purposefully share His love with you.

He gave His very life for you...and in doing so declared that you are worthy of His love.

Brian Fisher
Co-Founder and President, Human Coalition
Author of *Abortion: The Ultimate Exploitation of Women*

The Lord himself goes before you
and will be with you;
he will never leave you nor forsake you.

- Deuteronomy 31:8

A Mother's Lament

by Shadia Hrichi

I placed her into the hands of wicked men,
   behind closed doors, they give birth to death—
     for a few coins, her name was stricken;
     for an ounce of silver, they blot out her name.
Deceitful women pour out words like honey;
   like a serpent, her mouth drips with poison—
     both rich and poor drink from her cup,
     she shows no favoritism.
Monsters! Daughters are led by the hand as a blind sacrifice,
   to a heinous god, they are laid out as an offering;
     in the cover of darkness, their children are taken,
     before the dawn, their light is remembered no more.

My friends demand laughter,
my mother asks for a smile,
   can they not hear?
   can they not see?
Within my heart, deathly silence pounds,
behind the teeth is caged a scream,
   it is ready to burst like the wails of a woman in labor—
   like a mother whose child is stillborn.
"Weeds!" the wicked cry out as the sickle slashes the lilies;
tender violets are trampled and the garden destroyed,
   so that no fruit blossoms,
   no flower takes root.

I spend my days in masked despair,
in plain sight, I veil empty arms;
   shielding my ears from the haunting silence
   as vacant cries kick and fret within me.
As frightened deer scatter, my youth quickly fades;
As the morning delivers the moon, my days give birth to years—
   until I can no longer discern:
   are these my cries, Lord, or yours?

Who will kneel alongside me in the garden,
or climb upon my shoulders and fill my basket?
Who will lead me by the hand when I am gray,
or lay flowers at my grave?
A thousand tithes cannot repay my debt,
ten thousand offerings cannot restore a single breath;
don't turn your eye from my presence, Oh Lord,
don't close your ear to my cry.
The godless promise shelter to the abandoned,
they set a snare for those seeking refuge—
the frightened who have no one to take their hand
and lead them to your courts.

Oh Righteous Judge, give the wicked wrath to drink,
may blood blanket the graves of the unrighteous!
May those who say, "There is no God" shudder at the
thunder of your voice,
and tremble at the words of your mouth.
Your decrees are just and your law is perfect.
Cleanse me, Oh Lord, from my sin—
do not blot my name from your book,
do not strike my name with your pen.
You, Oh Lord, are my deliverer;
You, Oh God, are my strength.
With lifted hands, I will praise you to the congregation.
I will speak of your mercy, my God, my Savior.

Note: Some names have been changed and situations altered to protect privacy.

One

The Lie

A chorus of lockers rattled and slammed as the morning bell prodded a herd of high-schoolers into something resembling Spain's running of the bulls. I raced down the hallway. Clutching my knapsack in one hand with the other clenched over my mouth, I zigzagged around the mob of kids scrambling to get to their classrooms. Bursting into the nurse's office, I made a beeline for the restroom, locked the door, and braced myself over the toilet. Seconds later, the vomiting started—again. Yesterday, I made it as far as the wastebasket. The day before was not a pretty sight.

My fingers fumbled to flush the toilet before I slumped against the cool, damp wall. Several minutes passed before I gathered my strength to steady myself at the sink and let loose some cold water. A sharp shrill behind the wall betrayed the protest of the school's aging pipes. The teakettle-like scream sent a shooting pain across my brow. Shutting my eyes only made it worse. The room seemed to spin and I latched onto the edge of the sink like the safety bar on a carnival ride.

When I opened my eyes, I hardly recognized the reflection in

1

the mirror. My face was devoid of color save for the faint black and purple racing stripes left by my eye makeup. I felt something touch the tips of my fingers. I looked down. The running water had begun to form a small pool. Releasing my strangle-hold on the sink's rim, I scooped up a handful of water and gargled in a feeble attempt to erase the foul vomit taste clinging to my mouth.

Beads of sweat clamored down my neck. Using a wad of dampened paper towels, I chased after them. When I had regained some semblance of composure, I eased open the door and peered down the hall. It was deserted. Momentarily relieved, I picked up my knapsack and inched toward the front office.

I darted past the nurse who tended to a young boy with a bloody nose.

"I phoned your mother," she called out after me, "she's on her way to pick you up."

Stealing a glance over my shoulder, I saw the nurse shake her head as she plopped a blood-soaked bandage into the trash with a soggy-sounding plunk. The nasty sound threatened my stomach with a replay. I hurried out of the office and waited in the school's parking lot for my mom to arrive.

Not knowing what was wrong she had arranged an appointment with our family doctor. After a brief exam and some questioning, the doctor spoke privately with my mother. We left his office and my mother drove us to the local Planned Parenthood—the same clinic she and I visited just six months earlier to obtain the protection we assumed I'd soon need. Hesitant to trade the familiar street noises for what might lie ahead, I trailed inside the building behind my mother needing, but dreading, an answer.

In the lobby, a bright bouquet of artificial flowers adorned the large reception desk. Seated behind it was the receptionist, who was busy filling out forms. Still-life paintings disguised the windowless walls while a faint scent of lilac-laced Lysol dusted the air. Although my mind whirled with questions, the reticent atmosphere beckoned me to keep my thoughts and fears to myself.

"Please spell your name, last name first," the receptionist prompted, poising her pen over a legal pad.

"H-R-I-C-H-I," I responded slowly, always mindful of my name's unusual spelling.

After scribbling my name, she gently shoved herself, still seated in her chair, away from the desk, rolling across the vinyl tile floor to a nearby cabinet. She stood up and rifled through the files.

"Shadia?" she queried, as if there could be more than one.

"Yes."

After retrieving my thin manila folder, she encouraged my mother and I to take a seat.

We made our way to two vacant burgundy-upholstered chairs as the receptionist softly hummed to a tune playing on the radio. Not long after we sat down, a cheery voice pierced my thoughts.

"Miss . . . uh . . . Rich-ee?"

I looked up, accustomed to hearing my name mispronounced.

"Please follow me," urged a woman in a white lab coat.

I couldn't move. My legs felt anchored to the floor. My mom waited for me to gather my courage. Eventually, I stood up and we followed the woman to a back room. Inside stood Danielle, according to the block letters on her nametag, who motioned me toward a gray chair with an elevated armrest.

"Please sit down and roll up your sleeve."

Angry and scared, I shot my mother an accusatory glance, as if this were somehow entirely her fault. Danielle tied the thick rubber tubing around my upper arm. Two latex covered fingers tapped the inside of my elbow, coaxing the vein to surface. The noxious vapor from the alcohol-soaked cotton made me sick to my stomach. I turned away, unable to watch as the needle pierced my skin, and blood drained into the small cylinder.

"All finished," Danielle chirped as she tugged loose the rubber strap from my arm and whisked away the sated tube. "Now, let's get you seated somewhere more comfortable while we run some tests."

Moments later, I found myself in a small, windowless office sitting opposite a massive wooden desk. Danielle turned to leave and before she closed the door behind her, assured my mother and I that someone would be right with us. My mom sat in the chair next to me, looking anxious but saying nothing.

I scanned the room, looking for a distraction. The elaborately-carved desk displayed few objects: a small lit task lamp, several stylish pens in a wooden container, a stack of papers neatly tucked to one side, and a nameplate with the words "Angela Gerret, Director."

Straight ahead, a dark, immense clock hung on the olive green wall. Immediately, I honed in to the hollow ticking. In front of me, beneath the lamp's tranquil glow, delicate dust particles danced to a melody all their own as the clock above obediently marched on its assigned course.

A polite rap echoed at the door. Ms. Gerret, dressed in an stylish gray suit over a red silk blouse, came inside. Taking her seat in the bulky leather chair, her blank expression told us nothing. "Good afternoon. I'm Angela Gerret." She spread my file underneath her hands and announced, "The results are positive."

I breathed a sigh of relief, sending the flecks of dust into a tailspin. Positive is good, right? My ignorance obviously exposed, Ms. Gerret glanced at my mother then looked directly at me and said plainly,

"You're pregnant."

A dry film tightened over my lips as a foul, unfamiliar taste invaded my mouth. Saliva pumped feverishly to counter the strange reaction. A knot swelled in my throat, instantly taking my voice prisoner. I stared at the woman hoping I'd suddenly be struck with an ability to read lips. Jumbled words pierced my ears like tiny darts.

" . . . estimate . . . eleven weeks . . . consider abortion . . . schedule immediately."

I tried to focus.

"To handle the problem after twelve weeks," Ms. Gerret continued, as if scheduling a hair appointment, "will cost a lot more as the procedure becomes . . . well . . . more complicated." My forehead throbbed as I tried to make sense of her words. I slid further back in my chair.

Ms. Gerret reached her hands across the desk, gesturing for me to do the same. Slowly, I leaned forward. She cupped my hands in hers and lowered her voice, "Look, accidents happen sometimes. We understand that. That is why we want to help. When you are ready to have children someday, we will be here for you then, too."

I wanted to believe her. I knew I wasn't ready. Still holding one hand over both of mine, she retrieved a form from the stack of papers on her desk. "Simply sign here. It will be over in no time and then you can get on with your life. After all, you are only fifteen years old."

No one mentioned baby, child, unborn, ultrasound, heartbeat, life, death, grief, pain, loss, or regret. No one told me I'd have regrets. Regret that I didn't ask for more time. Regret that no one talked to me about adoption. Regret that I would later discover this would be the only child ever conceived in me. Regret that would propel a friendly, optimistic straight-A student into withdrawal, suicidal thoughts, and drug and alcohol abuse in less than a year.

We left Ms. Gerret's office with an appointment scheduled for Saturday.

Reflection Questions

I. Lies

I believed the lies. I thought having an abortion would allow me to get on with my life. But life after the abortion was never the same. Listed below are some of the changes I experienced and their impact although at the time, I did not recognize them as related to the abortion.

Before	After	Impact
Straight-A student	Got involved with wrong crowd, started abusing drugs & alcohol	Loss of self-esteem
One steady relationship	Promiscuous, one-night stands	Loss of self-respect
Close friendships	Withdrawn, Keeping secrets	Built "walls" around my heart

1. On the following two pages, describe in what ways your life changed after the abortion.

   a. List some before and after changes in the first and second columns. (such as likes/dislikes, personality or behavioral changes)

   b. Then, in the last column, write what you believe changed internally (such as emotionally, psychologically, or spiritually).

Impact

After

Before

Impact

After

Before

Perhaps, like me, you believed a number of lies about yourself, your pregnancy…even God.

In Beth Moore's study *Breaking Free*, I learned that in order to remove the hold lies have on us, whatever they may be, we must develop the habit of replacing lies with the Truth of God's Word—and we must do this continuously until the lie no longer has any power over us.

2. In Romans 12:2, the apostle Paul writes, *"Do not be conformed any longer to the pattern of this world but be transformed by the renewing of your mind."* In your own words, how would you define each of the following:

   a. *CONFORM*:

   b. *PATTERN*:

   c. *TRANSFORM*:

   d. *RENEW*:

3. Based on the definitions you provided, re-write the meaning of Romans 12:2 in your own words:

4. What new insights did you gain?

On the next several pages, I've listed some of the lies I believed about my pregnancy, God, and even myself. Considering each set of lies separately (pregnancy, God, myself), I've replaced several of the lies we commonly believe with the truth from God's Word.

Take a few moments to meditate on each set of verses before answering the questions that follow.

Lies about Pregnancy

Lie	Truth
It's not human *or* It's a glob of tissue	*"For you created my inmost being; you knit me together in my mother's womb. I praise you because I am fearfully and wonderfully made..."* Psalm 139:13-14[1] *"My frame was not hidden from you when I was made in the secret place... Your eyes saw my unformed body; all the days ordained for me were written in your book before one of them came to be."* Psalm 139:15-16[1]
It's not a person	*"Before I formed you in the womb I knew you."* Jeremiah 1:5 ESV[1] *"...The Lord called me before my birth; from within the womb, He called me by name."* Isaiah 49:1 NLT[1]

[1] selected

5. Without looking at the prior page (as much as possible), list as many key thoughts you can remember from the verses:

6. Is there one verse that is especially meaningful to you? Write it below and share your thoughts.

7. Make it personal: for each verse on page 11, circle every personal pronoun where the writer is referring to himself (rather than God), such as "me, my, I, you."

    a. Re-read each verse out loud, replacing each circled word with your own name (you will need to make some minor grammatical adjustments as you read).

    For example,

    "Before I formed [your name] in the womb I knew her."

8. Which Scripture(s) speaks to your heart the most? Write it below and share your thoughts.

9. Can you think of any other lies about pregnancy you have believed? List them here:

I was 11 weeks pregnant when I had an abortion. I was told it was nothing but a glob of cells.

10. How far along were you in your pregnancy? (okay to estimate)

11. What did you believe about the stage of your pregnancy at that time?

Lies about God

12. After reading each lie in the left column, look up the associated verses in your Bible (or on the Internet, such as www.biblegateway.com). Fill in the blanks with God's truth using the key words.

BRING   REMOVED   SEPARATE   PURIFY

Lie	Truth
God cannot forgive the *sin* of abortion	"If we confess our sins, he is faithful and just and will forgive us our sins and _____ us from all unrighteousness." -1 John 1:9 "as far as the east is from the west, so far has he _____ our transgressions from us." -Psalm 103:12
God cannot forgive *me*	"For Christ died for sins once for all, the righteous for the unrighteous, to _____ you to God. He was put to death in the body but made alive by the Spirit" -1 Peter 3:18 "For I am sure that neither death nor life, nor angels nor rulers, nor things present nor things to come, nor powers, nor height nor depth, nor anything else in all creation, will be able to _____ us from the love of God in Christ Jesus our Lord." -Romans 8:38-39 ESV

13. For each of the previous verses, circle every personal pronoun where the writer is referring/including himself (rather than God), such as "our, us, we, you."

    a. Re-read each verse out loud, replacing each circled word with your own name (you will need to make some minor grammatical adjustments as you read).

14. What one thing does the passage say that is especially meaningful to you? Write it below and share your thoughts.

15. Can you think of any other lies about God you have believed? Explain.

How do you suppose they could have developed?

What impact might they have had on your relationship with Him?

Lies about Myself

Reflect on the following verses and the lies they dispel.

Lie	Truth
My heart is too hardened; I cannot be healed	*"And I will give you a new heart, and a new spirit I will put within you. And I will remove the heart of stone from your flesh and give you a heart of flesh."* -Ezekiel 36:26 ESV *"Therefore, if anyone is in Christ, the new creation has come: The old has gone, the new is here!"* -2 Corinthians 5:17
I'm forgiven but unworthy to serve God	*"For we are God's workmanship, created in Christ Jesus to do good works, which God prepared in advance for us to do."* -Ephesians 2:10 *"And we know that for those who love God all things work together for good, for those who are called according to his purpose."* -Romans 8:28 ESV

16. Once more, let's make it personal. For each verse, circle the pronouns where the writer is referring to either himself or the reader (rather than God), such as "you, anyone, those."

    a. Re-read each verse out loud, replacing each circled word with your name and making adjustments as needed.

17. Which Scripture(s) is/are especially meaningful to you? Share your thoughts.

18. Look back at the last two verses; how does the author reveal his unwavering assurance in God's sovereignty and faithfulness?

The words of Scripture are powerful. If you struggle to believe that God is able to use you, consider praying these verses back to God.

19. Can you think of any other lies about yourself that you have believed? List them below and why you think they persisted.

Very often, the lies we believe about either ourselves or God both center on self: my heart, my sin, my unworthiness…but being forgiven, healed, and delivered are not based on our own efforts or goodness . . . they are possible only because of the grace of God and His work on the Cross. The question we have to ask ourselves is whether we really believe this.

Perhaps you've been trying to live a good, moral life, or trying to earn God's favor as a successful career woman, super-mom, or super-Christian.

20. Ask God to reveal to you if you've been trying to add your own efforts to God's perfect gift. If so, write your efforts here:

Perhaps instead of (or in addition to) trying to add your efforts onto God's perfect work, you impose imagined limits on Him: *God can't heal me, God can't forgive me…*or

21. Complete the sentence:

God can't …

Dear daughter of the King,

God is all-powerful; there is only one thing God cannot do and that's sin. When we place limits on God, or try to add to Jesus' work on the Cross, we are being deceived by the same lie: He's not enough.

Take a few moments to search your heart and ask God if there is something He wants you to confess. In surrendering our struggles to God, we can re-discover the joy of knowing He is enough. If you choose, record your thoughts below.

Lesson Summary:

At the end of each lesson, you will be asked to select a favorite Scripture, statement, or thought that was most significant to you, and to write it both in the workbook and also onto a notecard. Commit to keep the notecards in a place where you can refer to them often (such as your Bible or purse). You may also want to record them in your phone or tablet; however, do not neglect to hand-write them as this has been proven to reinforce memory retention. Starting today, and with your first note card which you will complete shortly, begin to commit them to memory.

What Scripture, statement, or thought was most significant to you? Write it below and also on your first notecard.

Re-word the Scripture or statement into a prayer of response to God.

Dear Sister, you finished your first lesson! You've taken a courageous step and have remained faithful. May God reward you as you commit to completing this journey.

Two

The Secret

"Time to go," mom whispered from the doorway of my bedroom. I rose from the edge of my bed where I was looking out the window at nothing in particular. After gathering my purse and jacket, I headed outside where the fog's thick haze choked out most of the morning sun. The crisp scent of looming rain followed me into the backseat of my step-dad's Pacer—a car I always thought looked like a UFO in a low budget movie. My mother slipped in beside him as he started the engine. As we backed out of the driveway, I gingerly rolled down the window, careful not to rip loose the old handle. Soon enough, a gentle rain licked steadily at the tires, the sound curiously reminding me of sizzling bacon. We drove in virtual silence for over an hour before exiting the freeway. We approached our destination and my step-dad eased up on the gas. A child shrieked playfully in the distance . . . a sinister breeze caressed my skin.

A feeling of dread slowly coiled around my chest as we entered the large facility. Just like at the clinic only days before, the silent waiting room betrayed its occupants' anxiety. Dozens of somber women and young girls, along with a smattering of boyfriends, friends, and parents, filled the room. No one smiled. No one spoke. We avoided eye contact. Meanwhile, my heart pounded faster and louder like the distant beat of a tribal drum.

We sat down. From that moment, it seemed that time had stood still until I heard my name butchered once again.

"Mizz . . . Reeshee?" a voice called out, "Please follow me."

I stood up—alone—and robotically followed the attendant down a narrow hallway. She paused at a small dressing room.

"Please put this on," she ordered, handing me a limp, colorless gown.

A thin film of perspiration glazed my skin. My fingers trembled and slipped beneath my long hair as they struggled to fasten the gown's ragged ties behind my neck. I believed that on this side of the curtain stood a scared, pregnant teenage girl but on the other side: my promised freedom.

The attendant's scrubs rustled as she shifted her weight from one foot to the other. Feebly, I tugged at the curtain, bunching it to one side, and followed the attendant down the brown carpeted hall. We passed several closed doors until she reached an open doorway and stopped, stepping aside so I could enter.

"Please come here and climb on the table," bid a nurse from across the room as she yanked several yards of crisp white paper across the long, metal table. My bare feet cringed as I stepped onto the cold vinyl floor. A disturbing smell instantly reminded me of the taste of dentists' Novocain. Climbing onto the table, I wrestled with the flimsy white paper shifting and tearing beneath me as slivers of cold metal stung my sweat-soaked skin.

I laid down, my heart beating faster and harder as I searched the faces of the nurses attending to their tasks on either side of me. Silently, I pleaded with them for words of reassurance but no one seemed to notice. Metal instruments clanged into position. Equipment whirred and hissed followed by a sharp "snap, snap!" as two steel arms were hoisted into the air.

I peered at the nurses chatting above me about their plans for the weekend. As if by reflex, one of them grabbed my hand just as the first spasms of pain hit. Though her gesture was hauntingly

cold, I clutched her hand tightly against my chest; it was all I had and I desperately needed to hold on to something . . . to someone . . . anyone. I stared at the acoustic ceiling tiles and was soon chasing the path of crevices hoping against hope they would lead me anywhere but here. My eyes slammed shut; it was no use. The sickening stench of fear mixed with rubbing alcohol and that strange Novocain-like smell merged into a nightmare. The steady convulsions of the suction machine throbbed inside my head, coaching my abdomen to contract alongside its sinister, pulsing rhythm.

I had no idea that in response to my body's release of chemicals due to fear, pain and stress, the beat of another tiny heart rapidly started to rise. A little body, already responsive to the stroke of a single human hair, jerked and twisted as cruel instruments took their aim, intent that no evidence of its existence would remain. A teeny thumb, upon which gentle sucking already began several weeks earlier, anonymously slipped away into the darkness as a flawless smile contorted into hollow scream . . . I can only ask now: who was holding onto her little hand?

At last, it was over. No name. No mourning. No record of her existence. Just biological waste from a brief medical procedure. After resting a short time on one of dozens of cots in a recovery room, I was escorted back to my mom and step-dad who were anxiously waiting for me in the patient pickup area, located at the rear of the clinic. I don't remember if any of us spoke. We exited the back of the building and started walking toward the car. Moments later, I keeled over with intense cramps. I clenched my stomach trying to wrestle it under control. A burning sweat percolated across my brow. Then, right there in the middle of the parking lot, I vomited.

When it was over, I leaned against the bumper of someone's Jeep Cherokee. To my surprise, I was neither embarrassed nor upset; my emotions had simply numbed. My mother hurried back inside the building where someone assured her my reaction was perfectly normal and handed her some paper towels. When the nausea dissipated, we resumed our walk to the car. We drove home in silence—a silence that would haunt my heart for the next twenty-five years.

On Monday morning, I walked down the small hill between our house and the school bus stop. I watched as the orange-yellow bus approached and came to a halt, greeting me with its hydraulic pop and sharp gush of air. The double doors opened. Slowly, I climbed the narrow black steps. Surveying the dozen or so faces, I was relieved to see that my best friend, who boarded the bus one stop before mine, was not in our regular seat. I sat down by myself, avoiding eye contact with the other kids. I never told anyone what had happened—not even my best friend.

Reflection Questions

II. Secrets

Harboring secrets is one of the easiest ways Satan keeps us in bondage. Many times, I wanted to speak up but did not have the courage.

1. When you learned you were pregnant, do you recall a time you wanted to speak up but didn't (or tried but couldn't)?

    a. Is there someone you wish you had confided in while you were still pregnant but didn't?

    b. Since the abortion, is there someone you never told about your decision but at times wish you had (or could)?

2. How long have you kept the abortion a secret?

How do you suppose our lives might be different if we did not keep secrets from people close to us? For example, I sometimes wonder what might have happened if I had told my father that I was pregnant (by that time, my parents were divorced). When I became pregnant, I was not aware that my parents faced the same situation when they were dating and my mother became pregnant with me. Despite their fears, my father encouraged my mother to choose life. Looking back, I can't help but wonder if he might have encouraged me to do the same.

3. How about you? How do you think your relationships might be different today if you had not kept the abortion a secret? Respond to all that apply:

- Husband/boyfriend

- Father of child (if different)

- Parent(s)

- Children

- Close friend(s)

- Siblings/relative(s)

- Pastor/minister

- Other

Note: if you are struggling with whether to tell someone now, share your heart with God and invite Him to guide your steps.

Let's take a look at two famous Biblical examples of sin, secrets, and God's sovereignty (this lesson requires more reading than the others but I promise it will be worth it):

EXAMPLE # 1

David: God's chosen King

Read 1 Samuel 16:10-13 below (or in your bible):

And Jesse made seven of his sons pass before Samuel. And Samuel said to Jesse, "The Lord has not chosen these." Then Samuel said to Jesse, "Are all your sons here?" And he said, "There remains yet the youngest, but behold, he is keeping the sheep." And Samuel said to Jesse, "Send and get him, for we will not sit down till he comes here." And he sent and brought him in. Now he was ruddy and had beautiful eyes and was handsome. And the Lord said, "Arise, anoint him, for this is he." Then Samuel took the horn of oil and anointed him in the midst of his brothers. And the Spirit of the Lord rushed upon David from that day forward. And Samuel rose up and went to Ramah. (ESV)

God sent his prophet Samuel to anoint Israel's future king. Most scholars agree David was likely an adolescent or young teen when He was anointed king (though he did not begin his reign until the age of 30).

Now Read the following segments of 2 Samuel 11:

In the spring of the year, the time when kings go out to battle, David sent Joab, and his servants with him, and all Israel [to war]…But David remained at Jerusalem.

It happened, late one afternoon, when David arose from his couch and was walking on the roof of the king's house, that he saw from the roof a woman bathing; and the woman was very beautiful. And David sent and inquired about the woman. And one said, "Is not this Bathsheba, ... the wife of Uriah the Hittite?" So David sent messengers and took her, and she came to him, and he lay with her... Then she returned to her house. And the woman conceived, and she sent and told David, "I am pregnant."

When King David learned that Uriah's wife was pregnant, he had his officer retrieve Uriah from the battlefield under the guise of seeking a report on the progress of the war. After meeting with Uriah and hearing his report, David encouraged Uriah to go home and rest, see his wife, and be refreshed. However...

Uriah said to David, "The ark and Israel and Judah dwell in [tents], and my lord Joab and the servants of my lord are camping in the open field. Shall I then go to my house, to eat and to drink and to lie with my wife? As you live, and as your soul lives, I will not do this thing."

Uriah was an honorable man and refused to be comforted while his men were enduring the harsh conditions of war. Realizing his scheme didn't work, David tried a second time, this time by getting Uriah drunk; however, Uriah still would not go home.

In the morning David wrote a letter to Joab and sent it by the hand of Uriah. In the letter he wrote, "Set Uriah in the forefront of the hardest fighting, and then draw back from him, that he may be struck down, and die."

...When the wife of Uriah heard that Uriah her husband was dead, she lamented over her husband. And when the mourning was over, David sent and brought her to his house, and she became his wife and bore him a son. But the thing that David had done displeased the LORD. (ESV, vv. 1-5, 11, 14, 26-27)

4. Review the Ten Commandments as written in Exodus 20:1-17. What sin(s) did King David commit according to Old Testament Law?

5. According to these passages, in what ways did David try to cover up his offenses?

6. In what way(s) can you relate to David? Have you tried to keep the abortion in your past a secret?

David later publically repented of his sins which is recorded for us in Psalm 51. He also went on to write most of the Old Testament psalms, poetically expressing his profound love for his Lord. Read Psalm 51 in your Bible (or visit www.biblegateway.com) and then answer the following questions.

7. Is there a particular verse or phrase that stood out to you? Share your thoughts below.

8. Have you ever confessed your regret or sorrow over the abortion to another person?

    a. If yes, to whom? (ok to use initials or other mark known only to you)

b. How did you feel afterwards?

Acts 13:22 says, "*After removing Saul, [God] made David their king. He testified concerning him: 'I have found David son of Jesse a man after my own heart; he will do everything I want him to do.'*"

9. In what ways does God describe David in this passage?

10. According to 2 Samuel 11, did David's sins of murder and adultery occur before or after he took the throne as King over Israel?

    a. Since God is all-knowing and knew David would sin, what do you think God meant by declaring David "will do everything I want him to do?"

EXAMPLE # 2

Moses: God's chosen instrument to deliver the people of Israel out of slavery in Egypt.

Read the following excerpts from Acts 7 and Exodus 2:

When Moses was forty years old, he decided to visit his own people, the Israelites. He saw one of them being mistreated by an Egyptian, so he went to his defense…Glancing this way and that and seeing no one, he killed the Egyptian and hid him in the sand. (Acts 7:23-24; Exodus 2:12)

When Moses realized his crime was found out, he fled to a foreign land.

11. What sin(s) did Moses commit?

12. According to these verses, did Moses try to cover up his crime?

a. If yes, how:

After forty years had passed, an angel appeared to Moses in the flames of a burning bush in the desert near Mount Sinai. (Acts 7:30)

13. Considering all of the verses together, at what approximate age did Moses encounter God in the burning bush?

Read the following excerpts from Exodus below or in your Bible (Exodus 3:9-14; 4:1-5, 10-13):

"And now the cry of the Israelites has reached me, and I have seen the way the Egyptians are oppressing them. So now, go. I am sending you to Pharaoh to bring my people the Israelites out of Egypt." But Moses said to God, "Who am I that I should go to Pharaoh and bring the Israelites out of Egypt?" And God said,

"I will be with you..." Moses said to God, "Suppose I go to the Israelites and say to them, 'The God of your fathers has sent me to you,' and they ask me, 'What is his name?' Then what shall I tell them?" God said to Moses, "I am who I am. This is what you are to say to the Israelites: 'I am has sent me to you.'"

...Moses answered, "What if they do not believe me or listen to me and say, 'The Lord did not appear to you?'" Then the Lord said to him, "What is that in your hand?" "A staff," he replied. The Lord said, "Throw it on the ground." Moses threw it on the ground and it became a snake, and he ran from it. Then the Lord said to him, "Reach out your hand and take it by the tail." So Moses reached out and took hold of the snake and it turned back into a staff in his hand. "This," said the Lord, "is so that they may believe that the Lord, the God of their fathers—the God of Abraham, the God of Isaac and the God of Jacob—has appeared to you."

...Moses said to the Lord, "Pardon your servant, Lord. I have never been eloquent, neither in the past nor since you have spoken to your servant. I am slow of speech and tongue." The Lord said to him, "Who gave human beings their mouths? Who makes them deaf or mute? ...Is it not I, the Lord? Now go; I will help you speak and will teach you what to say." But Moses said, "Pardon your servant, Lord. Please send someone else."

14. How many times did the elderly Moses seem to question or doubt God's calling?

15. In the end, what did Moses ask God to do?

16. Considering all of these events, did Moses' sin of murder occur before or after God called him to be leader over the children of Israel?

    a. Do you think this is relevant? Why or why not?

b. Since God is all-knowing and knew Moses had committed murder, why do you think God would choose such a person to lead His people?

And yet by God's grace Moses went on to lead the people out of Egypt, was God's instrument in the miraculous parting of the Red Sea, was entrusted with the Ten Commandments, and even asked to see and experienced the visible manifestation of the very glory of God (see Exodus 33:18-23)—and this bold request coming from a man who begged God to send someone else!

Clearly, God had a call on Moses's life and when Moses eventually cooperated, God invited him to experience things most of us are afraid to even dream about.

Let's do a quick review:

- Did David sin before or after God revealed He had a call on his life?

- Did Moses sin before or after God revealed He had a call on his life?

- Did David try to cover up his sin?

- Did Moses try to cover up his sin?

Did either David or Moses's sins, faults, or fears alter God's call on their lives or stop God from using them? Not at all! Don't you see? It does not matter if we try to hide our sin from God, or whether our greatest offenses occur before or after He draws us into a relationship with Himself; He has a plan for each of our lives, and nothing— repeat: nothing—will change that fact.

Our God is the same yesterday, today, and tomorrow. Just as in David and Moses' day, God calls people irrespective of age, past mistakes, fears, or failures—and He still does today.

"'For I know the plans I have for you,' declares the LORD, 'plans to prosper you and not to harm you, plans to give you hope and a future.'" Jeremiah 29:11

However, it is up to us whether we will choose to believe God and cooperate with His plans. Spend some time in prayer and ask God for the courage to claim the calling He has on your life. He loves you and has great plans for you. (Record your prayer below)

Lord,

Lesson Summary:

What Scripture, statement, or thought was most significant to you? Write it below and also on your next notecard. Refer to the cards throughout the week, committing them to memory.

Re-word the Scripture or statement into a prayer of response to God.

THREE

The Crossroads

I never told anyone. Not even my best friend…

That was twenty-five years ago. During most of those years, I avoided looking back, even after receiving God's forgiveness ten years ago. But not today. Once again, I found myself contemplating the upcoming abortion-recovery retreat a friend had persuaded me to sign up for. With the retreat still two months away, and after resisting the subject for so many years, I couldn't help wondering what was in store for me. My mind was restless.

The tension started building up weeks ago beginning with a conversation at church one Sunday in between the morning's sermon and Sunday school. I had just entered the reception area, pausing at the snack table to fix myself a cup of coffee, when Beth passed by.

I remember her once telling me she had attended the same retreat several years earlier.

"Beth!" I called out behind her.

She stopped and turned around. Hastily, I dumped three

packets' worth of sugar into my coffee and hurried over to her.

"Do you have a moment?" I urged, "I really need to ask you something."

"Of course." She smiled.

I lowered my voice, "You know that retreat you once told me about? The one for abortion recovery?" I paused, giving her a moment to shift gears. "I signed up to go. I'm nervous and wondering what it's going to be like. Is there anything you can tell me ahead of time . . . you know, something that might make it a little easier?"

She leaned closer and whispered, "You're going to be asked to give your child a name."

My body tensed as a silent wave of panic slithered beneath my skin. I swallowed hard before a faint "thank you" tumbled from my lips. I don't know what I expected her to say but I was certain of one thing: *that wasn't it.*

"Are you okay?" Beth asked, wrapping her arm around my shoulder.

"I'll be fine," I mumbled.

But I wasn't. Over the next several weeks, my mind refused to put the thought to rest. *How can I possibly name this child?* I never sensed a connection with her and, until now, hadn't even thought of her as a *her!* I didn't think of her as fully human, and naming her certainly never crossed my mind, not once. A name gives someone identity—something I didn't think she had.

However, at some point I reasoned that if I intended to go to the retreat, I'd rather choose a name now, in private and on my own time, rather than at the retreat on someone else's schedule. Somewhere deep in my heart, I think I always knew my child was a girl. In the past, I would forbid such thoughts to linger, but today I allowed them to brush past every raw emotion until my mind finally accepted what my heart has known all along: my pregnancy was a child and my child was a girl.

That's when I resolved not to treat the matter of giving her a name lightly. As eagerly as I first dismissed the idea, I now made it my mission to find her the perfect name. Her name will have significance—a name that gives her at least one small piece of dignity. After all, it is the only thing I can offer her now.

With newfound purpose, I switched on the ceiling fan in my

spare room and logged onto the Internet. I set out to research baby names and at first, it was rather fun. I looked up the meaning of my own name, amused by the memory of my mother assuring me, "Your name is beautiful! It means *Singing Birds*." "More like *Screeching Owls*," my friends would tease. I had to admit I always thought the meaning of my name was ironic considering the undeniable fact I have no musical ability. However, today I discovered my name could also mean *Beautiful Voice* (perhaps, as long as I don't have to sing in public).

I searched the meanings of my brother's name, my baby nephew's name, and names of other family and friends. Finally, I re-focused on my initial task. Not knowing where else to begin, I simply started scrolling names from the beginning of the alphabet. Suddenly, my eyes locked onto the screen. Every hair behind my neck sprang to attention as my hands hovered in frozen weightlessness over the keyboard. The moisture on my lips evaporated as I tried to swallow the words silently screaming from the monitor: "Anamika, meaning "Nameless." Who could possibly name their child *Nameless*? But before the question could escape my lips, an answer, even more horrifying than the question itself, pierced my thoughts. The truth, I realized, was *I had*.

I allowed the name to sink in. I knew I had just come face-to-face with something I thought I had convinced myself did not exist. Yet, a few strokes of the keyboard, a random web page, and three little words brought reality flooding to the surface: I had *already* named her . . . *Nameless*. Twenty-five years ago, I believed the lie that I was not taking the life of a child, *my child*. Today, I knew the truth: my child did live . . . and I let her die. And she died without a name. She became Anamika—one of the countless, faceless, nameless whose numbers only God could grasp.

I fell to the floor burying my face in my hands, "God, I'm so sorry; I didn't know! Please forgive me!" Tears welled up from the very depth of my soul. I allowed myself to cry, really cry, perhaps for the first time in many years. I don't know how long it took. Finally, drained of my tears, I collapsed back into my chair. I struggled to catch my breath. When the stillness finally returned, a gentle whisper roused my soul, "It's time to give your child a new name." No accusations. No condemnation. Only the overwhelming nearness of a tender, loving God.

Standing at the crossroads where my grief merged with God's forgiveness, I understood for the first time that God did not want me to condemn myself forever for what I had done. The abortion was an undeniable tragedy. It left one dead and another wounded. Nothing I do can ever change that. Yet, in God's infinite mercy, He showed me there is something, one thing, I can still do: I can give Anamika a *new* name.

Reflection Questions

III. Crossroads

For years, I did not feel grief over my abortion. Instead, I stuffed away my feelings and lived in a perpetual state of emotional numbness. If you had asked me five or ten years after the abortion how I felt about it, I would have said "I'm fine. I don't really think much about it." And it would have been the truth.

1. How about you? When you think about the abortion, would you say you are in a dry desert of emotional numbness, the blistery cold of overwhelming sorrow, or somewhere in between? I've drawn an illustration below. Mark where you sense you are right now.

emotionally
numb

overwhelming
sorrow

Explain:

I've traveled along both extremes and you know what I discovered? It's the same road. The road is called Grief. Whether you feel paralyzed by guilt or don't feel anything at all, both positions can keep you separated from the God who loves you.

But here's the good news! God does not expect you to jump the tracks onto a different road. He knows your need and He came down from Heaven to meet you right where you are. No matter where you are on the road of Grief, you can begin taking steps towards forgiveness, toward the *Cross in the road*.

The Crossroads—a place where God's forgiveness intersects our grief over sin—the place where healing begins.

"He himself bore our sins in his body on the tree, so that we might die to sins and live for righteousness; by his wounds you have been healed." 1 Peter 2:24

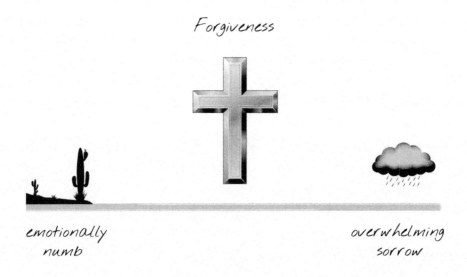

Forgiveness

emotionally
numb

overwhelming
sorrow

God desires to meet you at the crossroads – so much so, that He arranged for it before time began:

"[He] has saved us and called us to a holy life—not because of anything we have done but because of his own purpose and grace. This grace was given us in Christ Jesus before the beginning of time, but it has now been revealed through the appearing of our Savior, Christ Jesus, who has destroyed death and has brought life and immortality to light through the gospel."
- 2 Timothy 1:9-10

2. Have you ever experienced a time where you sensed your grief merge with God's forgiveness? Explain.

3. What does it mean to you to know that God arranged for the forgiveness of sins even before the world began--even before the first sin was ever committed?

One of the things I discovered as I began to put my story to pen and paper was the remarkable similarity between the things I felt had been stolen from the child I aborted—identity, significance, and dignity—and the things Satan had stolen from me.

4. In your own words, how would you define the following?

   a. *IDENTITY*:

   b. *SIGNIFICANCE*:

   c. *DIGNITY*:

5. Since the time of the abortion, have you sensed a personal struggle in any of these areas? On the following page, circle either Yes / No / Unsure for each area and share your thoughts in the space provided.

Worthy of Love

Struggle	Explain
IDENTITY **Yes No Unsure**	
SIGNIFICANCE **Yes No Unsure**	
DIGNITY **Yes No Unsure**	

I've listed six Scriptures below and on the next page. Although they're grouped into three categories: Identity, Significance, and Dignity, you will find that all three overlap and work together.

As you read through the verses, make a mental note of those which you sense God may want you to pay particular attention. Keep in mind that the verse(s) could be ones you quickly and easily embrace or possibly ones that trigger some discomfort.

Struggle	*Scripture*
IDENTITY	*"Therefore, if anyone is in Christ, he is a new creation; the old has gone, the new has come!"* -2 Corinthians 5:17 *"But you are a chosen people, a royal priesthood, a holy nation, God's special possession, that you may declare the praises of him who called you out of darkness into his wonderful light."* -1 Peter 2:9
SIGNIFICANCE	*"...when you heard the message of truth... [and] believed, you were marked in him with a seal, the promised Holy Spirit, who is a deposit guaranteeing our inheritance until the redemption of those who are God's possession—to the praise of his glory."* -Ephesians 1:13-14 *"For we are God's workmanship, created in Christ Jesus to do good works, which God prepared in advance for us to do."* -Ephesians 2:10

DIGNITY

"So God created mankind in his own image, in the image of God he created them; male and female he created them."

-Genesis 1:27

"Don't you know that you yourselves are God's temple and that God's Spirit lives in you?"

-1 Corinthians 3:16

6. Slowly re-read all six verses one time through. Without looking back (as much as possible), fill in the blanks:

a. I am God's _____,

   created in Christ Jesus to do good

   works.

b. I have been called out of

   darkness into His wonderful

   _____.

c. I am marked in Christ with a

   _____, the promised Holy

   Spirit, who is a deposit guaranteeing

   my _____.

d. I am made in the _____
of God.

e. Because I am in Christ, I am a new

_____.

f. I am God's temple and His Spirit
_____ in me.

g. I am among a chosen people, a
royal priesthood, a holy nation, God's
special _____.

7. Look back at the struggles you identified in
question 5. Select several verses that speak to you
personally. Write the Scripture references below.
Then, take a few moments to write out the complete
verse(s) on your notecards and add them to your
stack of memory cards as a reminder of who you
are as a beloved child of God.

Perhaps you are still uncertain of your standing with God.

If you are unsure you have ever placed your faith in Jesus, why not accept His marvelous gift of salvation right now? Romans 10:9 promises, *"If you confess with your mouth, 'Jesus is Lord,' and believe in your heart that God raised Him from the dead, you will be saved."* You can give your life to Christ today by praying to God, asking Him to forgive your sins, thanking him for sending His Son Jesus to save you, and inviting Jesus to be the Lord of your life from this day forward. Write your prayer below. (Don't forget to share your news with a friend, group leader, or another member of the study. They'll be thrilled!)

Lord,

If you previously accepted God's gift of salvation through the death and resurrection of Jesus Christ, share the time and circumstances surrounding your experience below. Follow it with a prayer of thanksgiving to God for His boundless love and faithfulness.

Lord,

Lesson Summary:

What Scripture, statement, or thought was most significant to you? Write it below and also on your next notecard.

Re-word the Scripture or statement into a prayer of response to God.

I'm so proud of you! You are nearing the halfway mark; don't give up!

FOUR

The Mask

A child without a name. No record of her existence. No acknowledgement of her life by her mother, family, or society . . . and, if the world would have the final say, no memory of her whatsoever.

But it's a lie. She did exist. She existed in my womb, experiencing all the wonders of life, as only the pre-born know it. She existed in the dreams of all the couples that were never granted the joy of caring for her. And she existed in the doctor's hands as he maneuvered his instruments in order to violate the very core of what should define a doctor's highest calling. And lastly, for the past twenty-five years, her memory has existed within my own heart, chained in secret captivity. I never knew this prison existed until the night of June 17, 2008.

The evening progressed like any other weeknight. Around 9:30, I opened the fridge, scanning its contents for something suitable to pack for tomorrow's lunch. Settling on a half-eaten tray of lasagna, I spooned a heap of gooey noodles into a small container.

After preparing the coffeepot, I poured myself a glass of water and headed to my bedroom. It was 10:07 when I set the alarm, switched off the light, and crawled underneath the covers.

Usually I fall asleep fairly easily, but that night I lay awake tossing and turning for hours. I recalled my last sleepy glance at the glowing red numbers; it was 1:33am. I suppose I fell asleep soon afterwards as I next awoke to the obnoxious "reep, reep, reep!" of the alarm clock just as I reached the end of a most disturbing dream.

In the dream, I had a bird's-eye view of a large children's playroom. Laughing toddlers scurried everywhere, delightfully chasing each other around the room. But something didn't feel right. I looked more intently but couldn't see anything. Nothing. That was it. Except for the children, the room was entirely empty: no toys, games, or crayons . . . no furniture of any kind. The gloomy gray walls were completely bare: no pictures, drawings, or posters . . . not even a clock. The carpet had probably once been a plush, bright blue but now appeared dark, stained, and dingy. There were no windows or doors.

By itself, the gray, windowless room should have felt dreary and sad but as I watched the children play, I couldn't help smiling. The children appeared entirely oblivious to the notion that their playroom lacked anything. I closed my eyes. *How long had it been since I soaked in such innocent joy?*

I heard a voice. Squealing in excitement, children thundered from every corner and rallied to the middle of the room. Many hopped from one foot to the other, wide-eyed with big, toothy grins. With miniature fists tightly clenched underneath their chins, they waited. Further enticing the children, the voice called out, "We're going to play a game. On the count of three, I want everyone to find a hug partner. Ready? One . . . two . . . three!" Like bursting popcorn, toddlers sprang into the air, jumping, laughing, and stumbling around the room in every direction, searching for a hug partner.

I closed my eyes, giggling to myself. When I looked again, I noticed a young girl standing in the center of the room with her back toward me. She wore dark blue jeans and a bluish-gray sweat jacket with the hood drawn tightly over her head. Although I could not see her face, her size suggested she was perhaps five or six years old, slightly older than the other children. Even in the midst of giddy toddlers leaping all around her, the girl hesitated with every awkward step. Turning guardedly from side to side, she seemed blind to the multitude of delighted children swarming all around her.

At that moment a little boy appeared dressed in a bright blue and yellow striped shirt and puffy toddler jeans that looked two-thirds rear-end and one-third legs. I guessed he was hardly three years old. His fair skin seemed to glow against his sleek, black hair.

The little boy bounced merrily behind the girl's every step. He tugged playfully at the hem of her jacket, confident she would pick him to hug but instead of turning around, she lurched in the other direction and then another as if searching for something . . . or someone. By now, the other children had all paired up, hugged one another and sat down, busily occupied with something else. Before long, the only children left standing were the anxious young girl and the dark-haired little boy. But she paid him no attention. The little boy trailed along behind her, the spring in his steps gradually fading, his playful tugs losing their grip.

Suddenly, the girl threw herself to the floor, locked her arms around her ankles and pressed her forehead into her knees. She rocked back and forth furiously as a sorrowful moan fought for an escape at every forward thrust.

Just then I found myself standing inside the room. I looked at the little boy fidgeting nearby. Burrowing his hands deep in his pockets, he glanced sideways at the girl. She was now lying on her side with her back toward us. He peered up at me; a pained expression marred his sweet face. I didn't know what to say. He slumped his head and shoulders forward and then drifted into the shadows. All of the other children were now gone as well. Darkness slowly crept inward. I looked over at the girl. The room was devoid of sound yet the piercing pain of the suffocating cries locked inside the little girl was almost deafening.

I stepped toward her and knelt at her side. Because I was facing her back and the hood of her jacket was pulled up over her head, I still could not see her face. Then, very gingerly, she turned toward me, but her face wasn't there! Instead, countless twisted cords lashed out all along the edge of the hood forming a mangled, hardened mask. The tightly pulled cords were so knotted that only two tiny, random holes remained, forbidding either light to enter or her cries to escape.

Her agony mounted, pressing harder and harder that I feared the depth of her torment would bleed right through the thick web of her prison. A downpour of tears spilled over my fingers as I leaned over her trembling body and slowly began untying the knots . . . then I awoke.

My emotions reeled as I replayed the dream over and over in my mind. Was the tortured little girl Anamika? Who was the little boy? Again and again, I played out the dream in my head. *The little girl just had to be Anamika, didn't she?* A lost child with no one to hug . . . cries without a voice? But Anamika is safe in God's arms, singing joyfully in Heaven. No, it cannot be Anamika. The little girl whose empty arms have no one to hold and whose cries have no voice . . . is me.

I slammed my eyes shut, trying to cage my tears. I thought about the dream, the little girl, the mask. In my mind's eye, I envisioned myself continuing to untie the knots. Suddenly, names began to appear upon the tangled cords: LIAR, MURDERER, UNFIT MOTHER. The more ties I loosened, the more appeared: BARREN, COLD, UNFEELING, UNLOVING! My eyes shot open. *Do I even want to go on?* Once more, I closed my eyes and grappled with the seemingly endless layers until finally, I confronted the biggest mangled knot of them all: UNLOVABLE.

Gingerly, I cleared away the last of the twisted, hardened web of lies. Just then, a beautiful bright light pierced the darkness. My heart raced. I mustered the courage to peer inside where I saw a little girl happily playing by herself, humming some nonsensical tune. Casually, she turned and looked up into my fearful, tear-swept face. For several moments, she gazed at me quizzically then simply smiled, "Hello, mommy."

My eyes flooded with tears. After several minutes or several hours, as the heavy load of my twenty-five year secret lifted off my fragile heart, I closed my eyes, and imagined myself looking inside one last time. Her face was so beautiful. Fighting back the tears, I opened my mouth to speak but nothing came out. I tried a second time. Nothing. Again and again, I tried to speak until at last, a broken, trembling cry tore past every layer of fear, guilt, and shame until I finally found the freedom to answer, "Hello, my child."

Reflection Questions

IV. Masks

Like most people, I tend to remember only a handful of my dreams and even then, few make any sense to me. Not this time. The dream where I saw a little girl trapped in a mask of countless knotted cords was as clear as it was heartbreaking. After I awoke, I was immediately grieved when I realized that the little girl with no one to hug and whose cries have no voice—was me. For many years, I managed to suppress the ache in my heart—even from myself.

1. Describe a time when an emotional wound was aroused that you hadn't even realized was there:

2. Do you believe you have suppressed your feelings about having an abortion? (Yes / No)

a. If you answered yes to the previous question, explain in what ways you have suppressed your feelings and for how long. Be specific.

3. In order to hide our true feelings, we may hide behind a mask (a false image that we project to others). If you have a mask, describe it below.

These things should not surprise us. The Bible teaches us in Jeremiah 17:9, *"The heart is deceitful above all things…who can understand it?"*

4. Re-read the above verse a few times. What thoughts or feelings does it arouse? Explain.

After I awoke from my dream, in my mind's eye I imagined various names written upon those twisted, knotted cords. Each was an accusation Satan had whispered in my ear at one time or another, which I had internalized into self-condemnation.

5. On the following pages, I've listed various accusations which we often use to condemn ourselves. Thinking back since the time of having the abortion, have you ever sensed any of the following accusations within your heart, mind, or soul? Circle either Yes / No / Unsure for each one and share your thoughts in the space provided.

Accusation	Explain
Liar **Yes No Unsure**	
Murderer **Yes No Unsure**	
Barren **Yes No Unsure**	
Unloving **Yes No Unsure**	
Cold/Unfeeling **Yes No Unsure**	

Accusation	Explain
Unfit Mother **Yes No Unsure**	
Unlovable **Yes No Unsure**	
Other: **Yes No Unsure**	
Other: **Yes No Unsure**	
Other: **Yes No Unsure**	

6. Do any particular ones stand out to you above the rest? If so, write them here:

7. Why do you think the item(s) you listed above is (are) especially prominent?

At the root of all of these accusations is Satan's attempt to strip us of our sense of self-worth, to keep us in bondage, and separated from God.

But please understand: God is not looking for sinless persons to embrace; He declared Himself, *"There is not a righteous man on earth who does what is right and never sins."*
-Ecclesiastes 7:20

Rather, His Word says, *"But God demonstrates his own love for us in this: while we were still sinners, Christ died for us."*
-Romans 5:8

He did this in order to set us free from the chains of sin and guilt that injure our sense of self-worth, keep us in bondage, and separated from God.

When Jesus was nailed to the Cross, He destroyed the barrier that previously separated us from God, *"But now in Christ Jesus you who once were far away have been brought near through the blood of Christ."* -Ephesians 2:13

As a follower of Jesus, when God looks at you, He sees behind the mask. You are His beloved daughter, holy and blameless in His sight, and when He looks at you, He is filled with compassion. It is imperative that we measure our worth, not based on how we see ourselves, but on how God sees us. God's love for you is not based on what you've done or haven't done, but rather on what Christ did on the Cross.

8. As a child of God, the Bible says you are:

Forgiven Blameless Sealed Loved Healed

Do you believe this? Each of these truths corresponds to one (or more) verse below. Identity the key word(s) that best match each verse then take some time to meditate on the Scriptures to remind yourself of what God's Word really does say:

Keyword	Verse
_____	*I have been crucified with Christ and I no longer live, but Christ lives in me. The life I now live in the body, I live by faith in the Son of God, who loved me and gave himself for me.* – Galatians 2:20
_____	*But God demonstrates his own love for us in this: while we were still sinners, Christ died for us.* – Romans 5:8
_____	*He himself bore our sins in his body on the tree, so that we might die to sins and live for righteousness; by his wounds you have been healed.* – 1 Peter 2:24
_____	*For I will be merciful to their iniquities, and I will remember their sins no more.* – Hebrews 8:12
_____	*And you also were included in Christ when you heard the word of truth, the gospel of your salvation. Having believed, you were marked in him with a seal, the promised Holy Spirit.* - Ephesians 1:13

But there's even more good news!

We have a hope and a future that has been promised to us *today*. The five previous verses represent present realities of how God sees us today.

The five verses that follow also represent how God sees us; however, because we live inside of time and God does not, we may not always recognize them as representative of how God sees us *today*. Consequently, we must **choose** to reject the masks and the lies, and embrace the truth of who God says we are.

9. According to the Bible, you are:

an Heir   Free   Chosen   Victorious   Made New

Each of the above five truths corresponds to one Bible verse on the following page. Identify which key word best matches each verse, and then take some time to meditate on the Scriptures to see what God's Word really does say.

an Heir   Free   Chosen   Victorious   Made New

Keyword	Verse

_____ *Therefore, if anyone is in Christ, he is a new creation; the old has gone, the new has come!*

– 2 Corinthians 5:17

_____ *It is for freedom that Christ has set us free. Stand firm, then, and do not let yourselves be burdened again by a yoke of slavery.*

– Galatians 5:1

_____ *...for everyone born of God overcomes the world. This is the victory that has overcome the world, even our faith.*

– 1 John 5:4

_____ *Now if we are children, then we are heirs--heirs of God and co-heirs with Christ, if indeed we share in his sufferings in order that we may also share in his glory.*

– Romans 8:17

_____ *But you are a chosen people, a royal priesthood, a holy nation, a people belonging to God, that you may declare the praises of him who called you out of darkness into his wonderful light.*

– 1 Peter 2:9

10. Refer back to question 5. For each accusation that you marked "yes" or "unsure," think about which of the previous ten verses best challenges each one (if another verse comes to mind, OK to use that one).

Next, one by one, strike out each accusation in question 5 that you marked either "yes" or "unsure" and write underneath it the word "Truth" followed by the corresponding verse reference you chose.

For example, if next to "Liar" the answer is "yes," then cross out the word "Liar," and underneath, you might write:

"Truth: Galatians 2:20"

11. Which of the ten verses listed in questions 8 and 9 resonates with your heart the most?

    a. Why do you think that is?

12. Take a few moments to write out the verses you listed in question 11 onto your notecards and add them to your memory verses.

This journey will lead us to new places, to a deeper understanding of the depths of God's love, and open our eyes to someone He wants you to meet.

13. Have you ever heard of the concept, or considered naming the child you lost to abortion? Share your thoughts.

Begin this week by praying and asking God to reveal to you the sex of the child. If you keep a journal, write down what you sense God is saying to you. Ask God to help you begin thinking of a name for your child. This is not always easy; it was difficult for me at first. However, it is an important step on your journey. Remember dear daughter of the King, you are not walking this road alone.

"For I am the LORD your God who takes hold of your right hand and says to you, Do not fear; I will help you."
– Isaiah 41:13

14. If you already have a name on your heart, write it below and describe how it came to you.

Lesson Summary:

What Scripture, statement, or thought was most significant to you? Write it below and also on your next notecard.

Re-word the Scripture or statement into a prayer of
response to God.

FIVE

The Stone

Often it's within the shadows of our wounded hearts where we will find our darkest secrets. Maybe it's something we're afraid to let go of . . . or a place we don't want God to look. Some of us have hidden our secrets so deep, only God can open our eyes to see them. He may reveal yours in a painting, through a conversation, or in a dream. For me, evidence of my secret first reached the surface the moment I saw her name: *Anamika*.

Less than two months later, God showed up once again in the most unexpected way. The weekend of the abortion-recovery retreat arrived. I printed out the directions and estimated it would take about twenty minutes to reach the Marriott Courtyard Hotel just twelve miles away. Figuring Saturday morning traffic would be light; at around 8:20, I filled my travel mug with coffee, grabbed my iPod and overnight bag, and headed out the door. Perhaps my favorite mix of contemporary Christian praise and hip-hop would help calm my nerves. The directions were fairly straightforward and in no time, I pulled into the hotel parking lot. It was now about a quarter to nine. I parked near the back, gulped down the last of my coffee and collected my purse and keys. I decided to leave my overnight bag in the car, just in case.

I approached the rear courtyard, greeted by the crisp scent of fresh cut grass and a sea of roses flaunting beautiful shades of lilac, pink, and coral. To my right, a dozen or so plush lounge chairs bordered the edge of a large pool. I paused to watch as a gentle breeze lulled the water into faint ripples. Above me, the chatter of birds' tweets and whistles were a welcome distraction from the anxiety churning within me. A budding pink rose caught my attention. I cradled it between my fingers and leaned in . . . perhaps its sweet scent could somehow chase away my fears. It did not.

I ambled toward the double glass doors presumably leading to the lobby. I imagined how nice the setting would be had I arrived for a relaxing weekend getaway. The birds and flowers faded into the background as each step carried me closer to the nameless fear I had been avoiding for so long. I reached the entrance. I closed my eyes and drew a long, deep breath before grasping the handle to step inside.

Two women immediately met me with warm smiles and outstretched arms. They introduced themselves as Lindsey and Karen, two of the three retreat facilitators, and brought me to meet Paula who cheerfully shook my hand and asked my name. She quickly scanned her list and presented me with a pre-printed nametag. Upon seeing my name spelled correctly, a nervous smile slipped past my lips. Lindsey then led me to a group of women gathered nearby. Placing her hand on the shoulder of a short woman with strawberry-blonde hair, Lindsey introduced us.

"Shadia, I'd like you meet Diane."

"Diane, this is Shadia. You and she will be sharing a room together."

Diane and I politely shook hands and exchanged small talk along with the other women. After several minutes, Paula announced that everyone was accounted for and invited us to follow her to the conference room. She, along with Lindsey and Karen, stood at either side of the double doors, welcoming us as we entered and handing each of us a brightly colored gift bag.

Inside, several tables had been arranged in a 'U' shape and

draped with soft, white tablecloths. Petite vases overflowing with dainty violet flowers marked each seat. Although I had no idea what to expect, the warm, welcoming atmosphere took me mildly by surprise. To my right, against the far wall, a table with coffee, tea, water, and a variety of pastries bid my further inspection.

I selected a seat almost within arm's reach of the tasty-looking treats. Peering inside my gift bag, I found a glossy, spiral bound workbook and pen, along with a crisp red apple (the red delicious kind, my favorite), a cranberry granola bar, a snack-size bag of potato chips, bottled water, and some cinnamon gum. When several of us realized our gift bags contained different snacks, we wasted no time negotiating exchanges.

"Would you prefer cranberry over that peanut butter granola bar?"

"You don't like sweets? How about trading my potato chips for your chocolates?"

In less than three minutes, my gift bag now included my original red delicious apple, two peanut butter granola bars, bottled water, and several bite-sized Snickers. After surveying my new assortment of goodies, I selected one of the crunchy granola bars, settled into my chair, and peeled back the crinkly green wrapper.

After the chatter subsided, Paula took a few moments to outline some logistics: the location of the restrooms, planned breaks, and what was for lunch and when would it arrive. Lindsey then asked us to review the Ground Rules typed inside the cover of our workbooks: do not interrupt another person who's speaking, be committed to keeping others' experiences confidential, remain non-judgmental, and so forth.

We then took turns introducing ourselves, sharing where we lived, and a few words about our jobs and families. When the tension in the room had eased, Lindsey asked us to share how many abortions we each had had and how long ago they occurred. Although I would soon discover it was I who had had an abortion farthest back in time (twenty-five years), I was surprised to learn that many of the women had come to the retreat at least eight to ten years afterwards; clearly, time had not healed our wounds.

Although the stories we divulged were painful, as I listened to the other women, I felt myself relax. It was the first time I had ever been around people with whom I did not have to hide the fact I had an abortion. Even Lindsey, Paula, and Karen revealed that they, too, had had abortions. And yet in many ways, we were a diverse group. Some had started families. One woman had recently reunited with her daughter whom she had released for adoption nearly twenty years earlier.

I described that at one time, I had been married and tried to have children; however, after a year with no success, tests revealed I had some damage that reduced my chances of conceiving. The cause was never confirmed. I confessed to the women that for years I suspected it was the abortion. Either way, my inability to conceive served as a painful reminder that I did something that should never have been done. Despite our differences, we all shared one thing in common: at one time or another, we each made a choice—and that choice changed our lives forever.

We spent the rest of the morning and part of that afternoon watching videos of men and women talk about their abortion and how the experience affected them, working through various questionnaires designed to help us process our own thoughts and emotions, and talking about how we felt before and after the abortions occurred. In one of the assignments, we were asked to draw a picture representing "My Abortion Scar." No other instructions were given. I looked at the blank page in my workbook and momentarily panicked, ever mindful of my lack of artistic talents. However, after reminding myself I could choose whether to show it to the group or not, I picked up my pen.

First, I sketched a picture of me smiling. My eyes were open and bright and I sported a big, toothy grin. Above the face I wrote, "Seen." Next to the smiling face, I drew another smaller face, representing what was "behind the Seen." This face had tightly closed slits for eyes and a straight-lined mouth sewn shut with about a half dozen stitches. Above this face I wrote, 'Unseen.'

Next, very faintly, I reproduced the 'Unseen' face inside the smiling 'Seen' face. The straight line of the closed, sewed up mouth matched the line on the smiling face where the upper and lower rows of teeth touched. The lines that separated the individual teeth on the smiling face matched the individual stitches sewed over the closed mouth. My jaw clenched as I stared at the image and confronted the depth of my pain for the first time: *behind the teeth was caged a scream.*

I swallowed hard, fighting back the lump swelling inside my throat. The women took turns sharing their pictures and stories. When my turn came to talk about my abortion scar, I realized I had already forgotten what the other women's pictures looked like. I decided to share mine. Since I couldn't remember what the others had shared, I realized that the exercise was not so much about sharing as it was about self-discovery.

Around three o'clock, we left the room for a short break before the last session of the day. A few minutes later, I returned to the conference room. Lindsey had just finished placing several softball-sized cobblestones on a small folding table. I guessed they each weighed three or four pounds. By the time the break was over, the others had all filed back into the room. Lindsey stood by the table with the cobblestones and waited until we were settled in our seats. She explained that the stones represented our "burdens"—the regrets, guilt, shame, fears, and emotional numbness we had been punishing ourselves with as a result of the choices we made. She asked each of us to come forward and take our "burden" back to our seat. When my turn came, I selected one of the remaining stones, returned to my chair, and placed it in my lap. Although unassuming at first, the stone's raw chill rapidly bore through my jeans and into my skin.

"From this point forward," Lindsey explained, "I'd like you to carry your burdens wherever you go for the remainder of the retreat—whether to make a phone call, visit the restroom, even going out to dinner—everywhere." Though feeling somewhat awkward at first, I soon became accustomed to carrying my burden with me.

At the end of a long first day, everyone looked forward to a relaxing evening. Our last session ended shortly before five o'clock and we agreed to meet in the hotel lobby an hour and a half later. I walked to my car, fetched my overnight bag, and used the remaining time to rest and get settled in my room. At 6:30, we gathered in the lobby. Paula informed us she had made reservations at Marie Calendar's, a local home-style restaurant famous for its fresh baked pies. The restaurant was only a few miles away and all we needed to do now was figure out who would drive. Although I enjoy driving my fun little Miata, because it's a two-seater, it's usually not much help in these situations. However, it turned out that after filling two cars, two of us would be left, making my car a perfect fit.

Heather, I learned, lived nearby and knew the area well. Because I am directionally challenged, I was relieved to have a navigator. We chatted along the way about our careers, where we grew up, and went to school. I discovered Heather was a kind-hearted person with a busy family, full-time job, and typical daily struggles. As we talked, a tiny ray of hope stirred within me; perhaps one day I will no longer have to hide the fact I had an abortion.

Arriving at the restaurant with our burdens in tow, it suddenly occurred to me that we must have looked like a bizarre Pet Rock Society. Thankfully, no one seemed to pay any attention. I assumed the staff had either been warned ahead of time or had been trained to never question customers' peculiarities.

Savory smells of meat loaf, gravy, and chicken potpie teased us as the friendly host led us to our table. We took our seats and neither the host nor the wait staff gave us a second look as we placed our large rocks either in our laps or on the table. While we surveyed the menus, Lindsey informed us that the rule of carrying our burdens everywhere would be suspended at the salad bar. A dozen heads immediately bobbled in agreement. Despite our heavy burdens, all of us enjoyed the tasty food, friendly conversation, and the chance to get to know each other better.

By the time we returned to the hotel, it was nearing ten o'clock. I, for one, looked forward to getting a good night's sleep. Instead, I found myself tossing and turning most of the night. The next morning, about mid-way through our second session, my thoughts began accusing me: *Why haven't you experienced the healing and hope you see blossoming in the other women? Maybe it's too late for me; perhaps my heart is too hardened and weighed down from so many years of carrying burdens of fear, regret, shame, and battered self-worth.*

It certainly hadn't taken long for the habit of carrying my stone burden to feel natural. At times, while listening to a discussion, if I had forgotten to place my burden in my lap, I sensed something was missing. Its absence had become as strange a sensation as when I placed it in my lap for the first time. I'm not sure which was more disturbing: the fact that my burden had become so familiar or the fact that it took only twenty-four hours to do so.

I looked around at the other women. *I wonder if I will get anything out of this retreat after all. Maybe I'm not ready. Or I just need more time.* Shaking my head as if to dislodge my negative thoughts, I reminded myself this is not the time to worry about it. I simply needed to give the retreat a chance. I directed my attention to the group discussion. Elizabeth, one of the ladies seated across from me, had just finished talking though I had no idea what she said.

Lindsey next informed us we would be given some time to spend alone with God to think about one thing we want to ask Him to do for us personally: our one "wish." Grateful to have a chance to get away by myself, I gathered my burden and bottled water, slipped out of the conference room, and headed to the beautiful flower-filled courtyard. I surveyed the patios and poolside before spotting a large flourishing tree in a secluded corner. A faint breeze tickled its leaves, beckoning me to come closer. I wandered over, sat down in the cool grass, and set my burden aside. Wrapping my arms around my knees, I lowered my head and closed my eyes.

Reflection Questions

V. Stones (Burdens)

    1. There is an age-old saying, "time heals all wounds." Do you believe that to be true?

        a. Why or why not?

Twenty-five years had gone by before I began to face the truth about my abortion. During the last three of those twenty-five years, it required the faithful prayers and gentle persistence of a dear friend before I finally found the courage to attend a post-abortion healing retreat. Some women experience instant grief and sorrow and seek healing within the first year. I waited twenty-five. Many are somewhere in between.

2. How about you? How long ago was the abortion?

3. After the abortion, was there a time you considered seeking help with any emotional, psychological, or spiritual struggles but were afraid to take the first step? Explain some of the challenges you faced.

4. If you did not seek help, what do you think prevented you?

5. If you did take steps in the past, do you believe
   they helped? Why or why not?

6. On the following pages, I've provided a list of
   some of the burdens women have reported they
   experienced after abortion (either soon afterwards
   or years later). Which areas have you struggled
   with? Share an example for each one you checked.
   I filled in one to get you started.

Burden   *Example*

Guilt   ☑ *When I learned I could not have
                children, I believed I was being
                punished for the abortion.*

Burden	Example
Guilt	☐
Regret	☐
Shame	☐
Emotionally numb	☐
Fear	☐

Worthy of Love

Bitterness ☐

Nightmares/ ☐
Flashbacks

Unforgiveness ☐
of self

Unforgiveness ☐
of others

Anger ☐

Resentment ☐

Grief ☐

Other ☐

Other ☐

What is interesting about our mental and emotional outlooks is that we're not always aware we have them. For example, I did not recognize that at the root of my emotional detachment were guilt, regret, and fear.

7. From the previous list, which particular issue(s) do you sense God is (or has been) trying to bring to your attention? Explain.

It could be that there is someone you still need to forgive. Many women struggle with the realization that they trusted someone, perhaps a well-meaning but misguided person (or persons), who had a strong influence in their decision.

8. Following are examples of some of the people whom other women have indicated were involved in their decision. Circle all that apply to you and write a few words describing how they were involved in your decision.

- Husband/boyfriend

- The child's father (if different)

- Your parent(s)

- Sibling/relative

- Friend

- Personal doctor

- Abortion/clinic staff

- Counselor

- Pastor/priest/ministry leader

- Co-worker

- Other:

- Other:

9. Among the persons you circled above, are there any whom you now realize lied or misled you (whether intentional or not)? Explain.

10. Is there someone that you have been unable to forgive? Explain.

If you answered yes to the previous question, ask God for courage and pray a simple prayer for this person (or persons). If you don't feel ready to forgive, ask God to cultivate within you the strength and courage to forgive. Remember, forgiveness is not a response to our **feelings** but rather, a decision of our **will**. We *choose* to forgive because Christ first forgave us.

"Bear with each other and forgive whatever grievances you may have against one another. Forgive as the Lord forgave you."
-Colossians 3:13

God desires to bring these things to light for one reason: so that in surrendering them to Him, you will discover the glorious mercy of His healing.

"He himself bore our sins in his body on the tree, so that we might die to sins and live for righteousness; by his wounds you have been healed." 1 Peter 2:24

Not all wounds result in tangible emotional, psychological, or spiritual pain. For me, not feeling anything at all was evidence of a very deep wound I wanted to protect. God knew my hardened and crusty scar was concealing very raw and painful memories.

11. If I asked you to describe your wound of abortion, what words come to mind? Without overanalyzing, list all words that come to mind in the space below.

    I've included a few of my own to get you started:

    Scar   Prison   Silence

Sometimes, heavy concepts are easier to process when we break them down. Creating acronyms is one way to reduce larger concepts into abbreviated, memorable forms by stringing together the first letters of each word in a phrase (think "FYI").

12. Choose several of the words you listed previously and create an acronym describing your abortion scar. For example, my acronym is SCAR, meaning:

    "*Silent Cry And Regret*"

    Now it's your turn. In the space below, play around with your words (or add new ones), combining them into your own acronym. (It doesn't have to spell 'scar' or even a real word, but it should be memorable).

13. During my journey, I shared how I was asked to
    draw a picture of my abortion "scar." What does
    your scar look like? Use the space below to sketch
    your own image.

Take a moment and write a prayer to your loving Father, share your hurts, your hopes, your fears, and your scars. Thank Him that "by His wounds, you are healed." (1 Peter 2:24) Let His healing touch wash over every one.

Father,

Lesson Summary:

What Scripture, statement, or thought was most significant to you? Write it below and also on your next notecard.

Re-word the Scripture or statement into a prayer of response to God.

Beloved Sister, if you don't yet sense progress on this journey, don't give up! As I shared in my own story, sometimes we need to be patient, giving God room to work. God has you on this journey for a reason. Keep trusting in Him.

SIX

The Battle

Cradled in my private patch of shade in the hotel courtyard, I wondered what kind of wish I should ask God for. Suddenly, questions I had avoided for years bombarded my mind:

Why, since my abortion, had I worked so hard to convince myself I never wanted children?

Why did I pass up chances to hold babies while others crawled over each other to get their turn?

When someone asked if I planned to have children someday, why did my heart turn cold?

Before I could wrap my mind around any one question, an assault of random memories invaded my thoughts. Years before, I burst into the emergency room with Tracy, a neighbor in the throes of premature labor. Attendants hurried her to a back room where the nurse swiftly applied a fetal heart monitor. Another snatched a nearby phone, punching the buttons to page Tracy's obstetrician. Just then, Tracy's sister Monica bolted past me. She reached the gurney and grasped her sister's hand, stammered that everything would be okay. Moments later, Monica shot me a panic-stricken glance. Tracy's sheets were drenched in blood.

Doctors raced into the room. Inching my way to a far corner, I wished I could disappear. *Why can't I go near her? Why can't I simply hold her hand? A child's life is at stake! Perhaps the mother's life as well! And I can't even summon enough courage to simply hold her hand?* My incapacity to help sickened me.

Childhood memories joined in the frenzy. I was about eight or nine years old and our Girl Scout troop had planned a weekend camping trip. My mom had arranged with the troop leaders for all of us to be at my house the Saturday morning before we were to leave. My fellow scouts and I were laughing and giggling in the living room when we caught a whiff of warm cinnamon. Scurrying to the kitchen, we found my mom elbow-deep in oven mitts removing a dozen steamy rolls from the oven. She handed us each a paper plate, onto which she delighted in plopping huge, grapefruit-sized cinnamon rolls. A pudgy tub of white frosting beckoned to us from the kitchen table.

Scrambling into our seats, we dove our plastic knives into the gooey fluff, smothering our piping hot cinnamon rolls until the icing oozed down the sides and all over our plates. I remember looking up at my mother and thinking *I am so lucky!* as the tip of my tongue frolicked on the hunt for the sticky warmth dribbling down the corners of my mouth. Mom beamed from the doorway; her treat was clearly a hit.

Before I could sort through these emotions, I saw myself at perhaps six years old. My mother had worked for weeks sewing my Halloween costume until at last, the long-awaited day arrived. She dressed me in my full-length black witch costume, painted my face green, and topped it all off with a big, black pointy hat. I was so excited I could hardly stand still. After she finished the final touches and was satisfied everything was perfect, she let me loose to run into the bathroom where I took one look in the mirror and burst into tears. Bewildered, my mother rushed to my side.

"Sweetheart, what's wrong?"

Frightened and sobbing uncontrollably, I stammered, "Mommy, I'm ugly!"

She didn't remind me I asked to be a witch. She didn't try to talk me into appreciating the costume she had worked so hard to create. She didn't even scold me for the likelihood this would make us all late for the party. I only remember her tenderly bending down to ask me one question.

"Honey, what do you want to be?"

"A princess," I sniveled as she wiped away my tears.

She must have performed a mental inventory of all her sewing and craft supplies before looking back into my tear-swept face. "How about I make you into a beautiful bride?" To this day, I still don't know how she transformed her black-caped, green-streaked, sad little witch into a happy white-laced, flower-laden bride . . . and we still arrived in plenty of time to enjoy the party.

After my abortion, however, those very same memories only brought guilt. When I would think back on mom's smile as she served the fresh-baked cinnamon rolls, or her gentle touch as she wiped away her green little witch's tears, the memories twisted into angry accusations. *You'll never be a good mother. You aborted your own child; you can never be trusted with children.*

I remember how, over the years that followed, to avoid the pain, I eventually convinced myself I didn't want to be a mother. If a joyful childhood memory slipped through, especially one with my mother, I would quickly dismiss it, condemning myself. *I'll never do that. I'm simply not the mother type. It doesn't matter; I don't like kids that much anyway.*

I was too young to understand that within my heart a battle raged. Twenty-five years later, in that small hotel courtyard, it had finally reached its peak. It was a battle between what I wanted to be (a kind and loving person) and what I believed I had become (someone without capacity to love). I had succeeded in exchanging the truth of my desire to love children for a lie that I didn't really want to be a mother. After all, it was far more bearable to believe that not wanting to be a mother was, in fact, *my choice.*

As the years passed, in order to fit into the new world my choice had created, I had to make other adjustments as well. In my heart, I know a mother should love her child. But when I chose abortion, I had to believe a **lie** (my pregnancy was a meaningless glob of tissue) in order to avoid the **truth** (I murdered my baby).

Not only did I murder my child, the abortion simultaneously devoured my own childhood as well. It robbed me of joyful memories, peace, and my sense of self-worth. And for many years afterward, the abortion stole my capacity to have a close relationship with my mother. After the abortion, I isolated myself from other people. Even worse, I did not understand why I had become so distant and cold toward others. Eventually, to fit in, I learned to live life on the surface. Desperate to be loved, I recklessly became a friend or lover to virtually anyone who would take notice though I shared my heart with no one.

As I sat against that large tree, I could hold back the tears no longer. Painful memories, lies I believed, lies I created, grief for killing my child and grief for the distortion of my own childhood memories mounted within me until I reached the end of my strength. Surrendering to its cleansing power, I allowed the torrent to wash over me until the last of my tears were shed.

When my mind finally cleared, I ask myself one final question: If, twenty-five years ago, I truly believed that my pregnancy was nothing more than a meaningless mass, why did I burden myself with so many lies?

When I became pregnant, many people, including those closest to me, viewed abortion as a reasonable option in a desperate situation. The courts and abortion clinics assured us, "We are here to help you. You are free to make your own decision. It is not killing." Being young, panicked, and afraid, I believed abortion promised freedom. But it was a lie.

Over the years that followed, cords of guilt and shame tightened their grip around my heart . . . inch by inch . . . year by year. Since I had not been raised in any religion and did not believe in the existence of God, the feelings of guilt and shame only confused me. I sought relief in drugs and alcohol. I found myself depressed and suicidal. But why? My mind said that there was no God and there was no baby, so where did all the guilt and shame come from?

Twenty-five years later, I found the truth. Whether I had a conscious awareness that a child was alive inside of me or thought of my pregnancy as nothing but a glob of tissue, a seed of love had been planted in my heart: a desire to love my child. And nothing, even refusing to believe in the existence of Anamika or God Himself, could alter that truth. Nor could $100 and a visit to a remote clinic tucked deep in the woods of upstate New York.

It happened on a Saturday morning in early May 1983. Without warning, a little girl was ripped away from the life-giving safety and comfort of her mother's womb and thrust into the loving arms of her heavenly Father. As Anamika opened her eyes to the start of a new life in Heaven, I closed mine, sensing nothing but the cold lifeless table beneath me. That was the day when the seed of motherly love God planted in my heart just eleven weeks earlier began to die.

I spent the next several years mastering how to keep Anamika's memory hidden from the world—and from myself. Within my heart, weeds of lies, guilt, and shame slowly choked out any life left in that little seed. Over time, the seed withered and hardened until eventually, its decay spread through my soul like cancer. By the time I reached adulthood, I had completely lost the ability to fully open my heart to anyone—even myself.

It was then, hidden among the shadows in the farthest corner of the hotel courtyard, with tears streaming down my cheeks, that I suddenly realized what I wanted for my one wish. I wiped the tears from my eyes, drew several long, deep breaths, and splashed my face with what was left of my bottled water. After collecting my heavy burden and empty bottle, I rose to my feet and headed toward the conference room.

Reflection Questions

VI. Battles

For years, I struggled to repress the pain that accompanied my own joyful childhood memories, as Satan often used them to twist into angry accusations like, "You'll never be a good mother." In spite of convincing myself I never wanted to have children, there have been times I've wrestled with the reality that abortion robbed me of my only child. It wasn't until many years later that I recognized the connection.

1. Below is a list of some of the battles women have indicated they struggled with after abortion. Which ones have you experienced? It's possible that you never associated the struggles as stemming from having had an abortion. They may be struggles you faced in your past or ones you're still facing today.

   I've divided them into two types, physical or behavior based ("visible"), and psychological or emotionally based ("invisible"). For each one, check the box indicating whether you've ever experienced it in the past, the present, or never.

"Visible" Battles	*Past*	*Present*	*Never*
Barrenness	❏	❏	❏
Sleep disturbances/ nightmares	❏	❏	❏
Drugs/alcohol abuse	❏	❏	❏

"Visible" Battles	Past	Present	Never
Suicidal tendencies	❑	❑	❑
Promiscuity/sexual problems	❑	❑	❑
Avoid babies/children	❑	❑	❑
Relationship Issues (struggle with commitment/intimacy)	❑	❑	❑
Withdrawn/Secretive	❑	❑	❑
Parenting Issues (failure to bond/over-protective)	❑	❑	❑
Eating Disorders	❑	❑	❑
Abusive/tolerates abuse	❑	❑	❑
Multiple abortions/ pattern of crisis pregnancy	❑	❑	❑
Other:	❑	❑	❑
Other:	❑	❑	❑

"Invisible" Battles	Past	Present	Never
Repress memories	❑	❑	❑
Un-forgiveness of self	❑	❑	❑
Un-forgiveness of others	❑	❑	❑
Low self-esteem	❑	❑	❑
Bitterness	❑	❑	❑
Anger	❑	❑	❑
Loneliness	❑	❑	❑
Fear	❑	❑	❑
Intense Sorrow/Despair	❑	❑	❑
Depression	❑	❑	❑
Anxiety (helplessness/ hopelessness)	❑	❑	❑

"*Invisible*" *Battles*	*Past*	*Present*	*Never*
Self-condemnation	☐	☐	☐
Hardness of heart/ emotionally numb	☐	☐	☐
Other:	☐	☐	☐
Other:	☐	☐	☐

2. Did you learn anything new about yourself? Explain.

Note: If you recently or are currently experiencing thoughts of suicide, please take the warning very seriously and call the National Suicide Helpline (1-800-SUICIDE), and confide in a trusted friend, counselor, or pastor.

3. After the abortion, did you sense a change in your relationship with God? If so, how?

4. After the abortion, did you sense a change in your relationship with your loved ones? Explain.

5. Did your view or opinion about God, abortion, or motherhood change after having an abortion? Check all that apply. In the space provided, share how your views changed:

☐ God

☐ Abortion

☐ Motherhood

☐ Other

"Cognitive Dissonance" (noun, psychology)

I've always found psychology fascinating. I was in college studying behavioral psychology when I first heard the term "cognitive dissonance." Consider its meaning below:

"...the feeling of discomfort when simultaneously holding two or more conflicting cognitions: ideas, beliefs, values or emotional reactions." (Wikipedia)

"A psychological conflict resulting from incongruous beliefs and attitudes held simultaneously." (Merriam-Webster)

The most heartbreaking example that I remember most clearly described what happens to an abused child. The child must wrestle with the conflicting belief "my parents love me" and the reality "my parents are hurting me." In order not to abandon the need to believe she is loved, an abused child will often conclude that she must have done something wrong. This false belief that she is bad and deserves to be punished, while restoring balance to the child's psychological state, will tragically have lasting, harmful effects.

In my story, I revealed how cognitive dissonance affected my view of abortion: in wrestling with the conflicting ideas "a mother should love her child" and "abortion murders a child," when I chose abortion, I was forced to reconcile these conflicting concepts. In order not to abandon the belief that a mother should love her child and to free my mind from the notion I was committing murder, I had to accept the lie that my pregnancy was "a meaningless glob of tissue" in order to cope with my decision.

Lies often serve to protect us from the truth we are not yet ready, or willing, to face. Previously in Lesson One, I asked you to review some common lies about pregnancy, God, and yourself.

6. Look back at Lesson One and review the sections Lies About Myself, Lies About Pregnancy, and Lies About God, as well as any additional lies you listed in questions 9, 15, and 19.

   List each lie in the space below. Then, underneath each one, list the corresponding truth you may have been trying to avoid. I provided one as an example.

<u>*Truth and Lies*</u>

Lie: My pregnancy was a meaningless glob

Truth: God personally "Knits" us together in the womb

Lie:

Truth:

Lie:

Truth:

Worthy of Love

Lie:

Truth:

Lie:

Truth:

Lie:

Truth:

Lie:

Truth:

7. Lies keep us in bondage but because of Christ we can know the Truth, and the truth will set us free! Following are several Bible verses. For each one:

   a. Circle every variation of the word (or theme) of *Truth*.

   b. Underline every variation of the word (or theme) of *Freedom*.

"But now that you have been set free from sin and have become slaves of God, the benefit you reap leads to holiness, and the result is eternal life." (Romans 6:22)

"I am the way and the truth and the life. No one comes to the Father except through me." (John 14:6)

"If you hold to my teaching, you are really my disciples. Then you will know the truth, and the truth will set you free." (John 8:31-32)

"It is for freedom that Christ has set us free. Stand firm, then, and do not let yourselves be burdened again by a yoke of slavery." (Galatians 5:1)

"The Spirit of the Lord is on me, because he has anointed me to proclaim good news to the poor. He has sent me to proclaim freedom for the prisoners and recovery of sight for the blind, to set the oppressed free." (Luke 4:18)

Take some time to meditate on the previous verses before answering the following questions.

8. What new insights did you gain regarding:

   a. *Truth*

   b. *Freedom*

   c. *Truth and Freedom*

Sometimes, at the root of a lie there is a kernel of truth. Throughout the Bible, Satan is seen as twisting the truth of God's words in order to deceive and manipulate God's people. It took a long time before I recognized that at the root of the many lies I had believed about abortion, God, and myself, there was a kernel of truth.

In my own journey, I describe this truth as "a seed of motherly love" which I believe God had planted in my heart the moment my child was conceived as part of His God-given design. However, in my attempt to suppress the truth, lies sprouted.

9. Have you ever sensed a "seed" of love or attachment develop toward the child you lost to abortion? Explain.

10. Perhaps, like me, you may not have recognized it, or deliberately repressed it. Looking back, can you identify any evidence that has now come to light that this "seed" has been there all along? Explain.

11. Over time, I had allowed a number of "weeds" to gain ground in my heart including various lies, fears and even bitterness. Are there any weeds you have allowed to crop up in your own heart that continue to have a hold on you? (You may find it helpful to refer to the lists of burdens, battles, and lies in previous chapters). On the following pages, list each "weed" and then underneath, describe what you believe has been the outcome. I filled in the first one with my own example.

The Power of Weeds

Weed: Believed the lie that I am unlovable.

Outcome: Unable to open my heart to anyone.

Weed:

Outcome:

Weed:

Outcome:

Weed:

Outcome:

Worthy of Love

Need:

Outcome:

Need:

Outcome:

Need:

Outcome:

Need:

Outcome:

Dear Sister, despite all the lies we've believed and battles we've fought, even if we've hidden the memory of our child from our own mind and heart, God remains faithful.

"Can a mother forget the infant at her breast, walk away from the baby she bore? But even if mothers forget, I'd never forget you—never. Look, I've written your names on the palms of my hands." Isaiah 49:15 MSG

Lesson Summary:

What Scripture, statement, or thought was most significant to you? Write it below and also on your next notecard.

Re-word the Scripture or statement into a prayer of
response to God.

SEVEN

The Wish

When I entered the conference room, something was different. The lights were dimmed, and near the front, a wooden easel leaned against the wall. An embroidered burgundy cape with a hem of dark red fringe hugged the small frame. I slipped into my chair. After everyone had returned and settled in their seats, Lindsey recounted a story from the Bible, enriching it with beautiful imagery for our benefit.

A woman had suffered from menstrual bleeding for twelve years. She spent all she had on doctors in search of a cure, only for her hopes to be shattered again and again until ultimately, she was left penniless and alone. Then one day a man named Jesus, who the people rumored had come from God, arrived in her small town. She ran out to meet him but the swarm of people kept her from getting close to him. She searched for an opening convinced in her heart that if she could just touch Jesus' cloak, she would be healed.

The shouts and commotion merged into a dull roar as a horde of arms and legs snaked all around her, swallowing her into the crowd. Unable to see or breathe, the woman propelled her hand through a tiny gap. Fighting for air, she pressed her head through the opening only to get a glimpse of Jesus passing by. Hoping against hope, she thrust out her hand, but the force of the multitude pulled her back into its grip. She lost her balance . . . then collapsed. Her slender arm tumbled into the dusty street where the trailing fringe from Jesus' garment softly swept over her fingertips. Peering up from the ground, the woman caught Jesus' loving gaze as he turned to face her. The silence of a single tear caressed her cheek as she realized . . . she was healed.

After telling this story, Lindsey invited each of us to the front of the room, one at a time, to where the flowing red garment had been propped. Here, we'd have the opportunity to surrender our burdens to God and ask for our one wish. When my turn came, I stepped forward and, upon reaching the front, fell to my knees. I set down my heavy stone, locked onto the burgundy garment, and silently pleaded with God for my wish.

While wringing the thick, red cape in my hands, a dark image flashed in my mind. The object appeared small, shriveled, and hardened. I instantly knew it was a picture of my heart. As it came further into focus, I saw my heart as an ugly, rotted mass of darkness. My eyes welled with tears as I saw what my heart had truly become. More than anything else, I wanted a new heart—a heart that would not cower behind self-made walls of fear, serving a lifetime sentence as both warden and prisoner—but one that would courageously reach out to love people.

Still clutching the cape in my hands, as tears battered my knuckles, I asked God for my one wish. *Lord, I want a new heart.* Immediately, a gentle calm washed over my spirit; however, what happened next took me completely by surprise. I had heard of people having visions though I had never experienced anything like this.

I found myself standing in Heaven, surrounded by an unimaginable, glorious light. A perfect peace unlike anything I've ever known triggered distant memories of me as a small child listening to my mother tenderly sing a lullaby. Someone appeared in the distance. My pulse quickened. I knew it had to be God. He held something in His hands that looked like a polished silver tray. A small oval-shaped object rested upon it, glowing with a dazzling aura of yellow, orange, and red.

I dared to believe God had answered my prayer. He walked toward me. His smile seemed to dissolve the span between us, as if He had reached out and scooped me into His arms. I could hardly breathe. I took a few awkward steps toward Him. While we were still some distance apart, He stopped. A knot barreled into my throat. *Did God change His mind? Had He decided I was too unworthy?*

He turned to His side. A young girl was there. Too frightened to look directly at her face, I fixed my eyes on her golden-brown hair. Long waves bobbed playfully against the front of her delicate white dress. Just then, she pivoted on her heel and in one graceful sweep, stood facing God with arms raised high. God leaned forward and with the greatest care, placed the silver tray into her waiting hands. She turned to face me. I stole a glimpse at the little girl's face. Wide-eyed with excitement, she nearly danced toward me.

My mind began to race. *Is this?*

I swallowed hard. I couldn't even say her name.

Does she know what I did? I couldn't bear the thought.

Does she forgive me?

What will she say?

Panic-stricken yet powerless, I just stood there. The pounding of my heart seemed to echo throughout the heavens. Before I could piece together the countless reasons this little girl's presence terrified me, we were standing face-to-face. Beaming with delight, she lifted her arms toward me, sending a tiny wisp of hair fluttering past her radiant smile.

My eyes slammed shut. By now my heart was beating out of control. An army of thoughts charged ahead from every corner of my mind, colliding every which way like a maddening game of pinball. Clamoring in the dark, thoughts of guilt, shame, and fear tried desperately to rouse the voice that's been silent for too long. Still, I couldn't speak.

She didn't say a word. No accusations. No condemnation. No judgment, grief, or questions. Still too frightened to move, I gathered my courage to open my eyes for one fleeting moment, and looked into her angelic face. And that's when the floodgate opened. Life-giving nourishment of forgiveness rained down upon that forgotten little seed, unlocking a tender shoot of motherly love to bud within my heart. Then, like the knotted cords falling away from the hardened mask of the little girl in my dream, weeds of guilt, secrets, and lies were pried from my heart and cast aside, having lost their power to suffocate the truth any longer.

I closed my eyes, burying my face in my hands. The feeling of fabric startled me. I lowered my hands and opened my eyes. I remained there several minutes staring at the red embroidered cape entwined around my fingers as tears splashed over my knuckles. I knew what just happened was not a dream. I had just met my little girl.

Reflection Questions

VII. The Wish

God works in mysterious ways—and He rarely repeats Himself. Our experiences are unique to each of us and God knows how to best meet our needs and fulfill His purposes. The woman who touched Jesus wanted to be healed—but God wanted her to experience so much more.

"Daughter, your faith has healed you. Go in peace." - Jesus

The Bible story more commonly known as "the woman with the issue of blood" is reported in three of the four gospel accounts. While I used some poetic license for the purpose of sharing the story, now we're going to read the actual Biblical account. Read the following passage from Mark 5:24-34:

...A large crowd followed and pressed around him. And a woman was there who had been subject to bleeding for twelve years. She had suffered a great deal under the care of many doctors and had spent all she had, yet instead of getting better she grew worse. When she heard about Jesus, she came up behind him in the crowd and touched his cloak, because she thought, "If I just touch his clothes, I will be healed." Immediately her bleeding stopped and she felt in her body that she was freed from her suffering. At once Jesus realized that power had gone out from him. He turned around in the crowd and asked, "Who touched my clothes?"

"You see the people crowding against you," his disciples answered, "and yet you can ask, 'Who touched me?'"

But Jesus kept looking around to see who had done it. Then the woman, knowing what had happened to her, came and fell at his feet and, trembling with fear, told him the whole truth. He said to her, "Daughter, your faith has healed you. Go in peace and be freed from your suffering."

1. What discoveries can you make about the woman in this story?

2. What about her can you most identify with personally as she seeks to get close to Jesus?

3. Why do you think Jesus waited for the woman to reveal herself?

4. As Jesus responded to this woman, what did He reveal about His own character? List as many aspects of His character as you can.

5. What was needed to bring this woman to a point of healing? List the changes she would have experienced from that moment on. Be specific.

6. Faith is the needed ingredient in our own healing. List all of the changes and newfound freedoms that you can experience when you respond in faith.

Jesus could have let the woman slip away into the crowd as she had hoped but He wanted to leave her with something more valuable than physical healing; He wanted her to meet the *Healer*. Only Jesus could truly "free her from her suffering." He wanted to heal *all* of her: mind, body, heart, and spirit.

"Daughter, your faith has healed you. Go in peace and be freed from your suffering."

Faith is the conduit that bridges the gap between our need and God's desire to meet that need, whether the need is healing, restoration, redemption, or resurrection!

7. Is there a particular struggle you've been battling throughout this study? Perhaps a lie you believed, a recurring anxiety or thought, or feelings of betrayal by someone you trusted? Share your thoughts.

8. Write a prayer to God for the strength to surrender these issues to Him and for the faith to claim victory. He desires to set you free!

God,

9. Read the following verses out loud, two times each, and then:

   a. Circle each variation of the word (or theme) *Faith*

   b. Underline each variation of the word (or theme) *Freedom*

   "For the one who was a slave when called to faith in the Lord is the Lord's freed person…"
   (1 Corinthians 7:22)

   "In him and through faith in him we may approach God with freedom and confidence."
   (Ephesians 3:12)

   "Every child of God can defeat the world, and our faith is what gives us this victory."
   (1 John 5:4 CEV)

   "Daughter, your faith has healed you. Go in peace and be freed from your suffering."
   (Mark 5:34)

   c. Did a particular verse stand out to you? Share your thoughts.

10. What insights, encouragements, or reminders did you gain regarding:

   a. *Faith*

   b. *Freedom*

   c. *Faith and Freedom*

11. Read the following passage from Isaiah 61:1-4 at least two times through (three is even better).

The Spirit of the Sovereign LORD is on me,
because the LORD has anointed me
to proclaim good news to the poor.
He has sent me to bind up the brokenhearted,
to proclaim freedom for the captives
and release from darkness for the prisoners,

to proclaim the year of the LORD's favor
and the day of vengeance of our God,
to comfort all who mourn,

and provide for those who grieve in Zion—
to bestow on them a crown of beauty
instead of ashes,
the oil of joy
instead of mourning,
and a garment of praise
instead of a spirit of despair.
They will be called oaks of righteousness,
a planting of the LORD
for the display of his splendor.

They will rebuild the ancient ruins
and restore the places long devastated;
they will renew the ruined cities
that have been devastated for generations.

12. This passage is filled with promises! Which one(s) speak to your heart the most? Write them below.

13. What does the passage say that makes it so meaningful to you?

14. Plan to spend some time alone with God this week (at least an hour if possible). This may seem challenging if setting aside time to be alone with God is not a regular habit; however, it is absolutely essential. Just as we need to feed and care for our physical bodies, our soul craves to be fed and cared for by our loving, heavenly Father. As you prepare to come to Him, think about what "wish" you need from God. You may also want to review prior Lesson Summaries as part of your preparation.

Lesson Summary:

What Scripture, statement, or thought was most significant to you? Write it below and also on your next notecard.

Re-word the Scripture or statement into a prayer of response to God.

EIGHT

The Gift

*I*t could have happened to me. The year was 1967. Thousands of post-war baby-boomers were coming of age and ready for a change. Prayer in schools had been declared unconstitutional. Use of marijuana was skyrocketing while respect for authority plummeting. Mystic religions, the Woodstock Festival, and sexual freedom marked the climate of this generation. And although abortion was illegal, it was readily available.

In the midst of this Cultural Revolution, a young woman and her mother shared an apartment in Manhattan's lower east side. One morning, the woman broke the news to her mother, "I'm pregnant." Fearful for her daughter's future, her mother encouraged her to consider abortion. Before making a decision, however, the woman arranged to meet with the baby's father. Having no idea how he might react, she simply whispered, "I'm pregnant." Several minutes passed as the weight of my world—*my very life*—hung in the balance. Finally, my father spoke. "Let's get married." I shudder to think that three little words saved my life.

She said yes and several months later, at Manhattan's Metropolitan Hospital, she gave birth to a little girl. Fifteen years later, that same little girl found herself with a difficult choice to make. Only this time, no one spoke up.

There are many reasons people choose abortion: children conceived out of wedlock, parents young and frightened, afraid of what others might think or worried if they are ready to raise a child. Yet it was under those same circumstances whereby one particular child entered the world and changed it forever.

A teenaged girl was engaged to a good and honorable man. She was likely around fifteen years old when she became pregnant. In her society, she risked public disgrace, abandonment by her fiancé, and the very real threat of a death sentence. When her fiancé learned of her condition (and knew the child wasn't his), he hoped to spare her a scandal and planned to call off the engagement. But the Father of the child spoke up, "As [the fiancé] considered this, an angel of the Lord appeared to him in a dream. 'Joseph, son of David,' the angel said, 'do not be afraid to take Mary as your wife. For the child within her was conceived by the Holy Spirit. And she will have a son, and you are to name him Jesus, for he will save his people from their sins.'"[1]

If this had happened in our society today, most of us could not imagine encouraging Mary to have an abortion. Yet, the excuses would have been no different.

"You're not married. What will people think?"

"You're too young to have a child."

"Joseph is a respected man. He's going to leave you if he finds out."

"What will your father say?"

I believe God chose both Joseph and Mary because although they were not perfect, they loved God and were willing to suffer the consequences of obeying Him. What makes this "what if it happened today" scenario so frightening is not that Jesus may never have been born (for in the end, God's plans will always prevail); but rather that there would be some people genuinely convinced that abortion was the right choice. Someone else might say, "But that's only because they didn't know who the child was." *Exactly.*

This side of Heaven, we will never fully realize the losses

suffered due to our poor choices. There is always a price to pay. However, long before time began, God planned a rescue mission. Two thousand years ago, in order to free us from our tangled web of guilt, lies, and shame, God clothed Himself as a human child, was born into this evil world, and although He had done nothing wrong, willingly took upon Himself the death sentence we deserved. He could have walked away at any moment but He loved us too much to leave us in our hopeless condition. He even had compassion on those who carried out his execution. As the soldiers nailed Jesus to the cross, He cried out, "Father, forgive them, for they don't know what they are doing."[2]

That prayer was not only intended for them. Jesus offers it to everyone. All of us are guilty of His death sentence. It was for our sin that payment was required. Yet, for every person willing to come to Him, God offers a second chance.

I'll never forget the day I took God up on His offer. It was June 1998. With my face buried in the living room carpet, I prayed to God daring to believe He could hear me. I asked God that if He was real, to please hear my prayer which may have sounded something like this:

God, if You can hear me, please forgive me for living my life my way. I'm sorry for all of the mistakes I've made. Thank you, Jesus, for dying on the cross for my sins. Please come into my life and make me the person You want me to be.

At first, I wasn't sure anything had happened. However, the next morning, a peace unlike anything I've ever known washed over me. I knew the Creator of the universe had heard the cry of my heart. I had been changed forever.

To all who bring Jesus their pain, disappointments, addictions, burdens and regrets, He offers a second chance. Two thousand years ago, as Jesus hung tortured on the cross, dying for the sins of the world, three little words were carried away upon His final breath, "It is finished."

Just as three little words spoken by my earthly father secured my present life here on earth, three little words secure eternal life in Heaven for everyone who believes. But there is one difference: I wasn't given the chance to cry out for life while still in my mother's womb. Thankfully, someone else did. Thirty years later, I heard of another man who shook the heavens as He cried out in His death to save my life, *my eternal life*. Only this time, I had a choice: I could accept His gift of life or I could turn and walk away.

From the moment I accepted God's gift of eternal life through Jesus Christ, I've never looked back. Yet, in God's boundless gentleness and patience, He waited ten more years, when He knew I was ready, to help me face another truth. The time had come. The time was now. And the instant I saw her name, I knew: my daughter was real.

Even though I had long since accepted God's forgiveness, He knew I still felt I couldn't forgive myself. I still needed healing. On Sunday, May 3, 2008, during an abortion-recovery weekend retreat, I finally found it. Clinging to God with one hand while surrounded by the love and prayers of others on the same journey, I unlocked the prison doors of my heart. As I released the memory of my daughter to Heaven, the punishing shackles of guilt and shame fell off. *It is finished.*

Deep within each of our hearts, the memories of our children lost to abortion wait longingly for us to open their prison doors, for the day we find the courage to let go of our fears. Fears that one day our secrets might be discovered. Fear that perhaps, if we are willing to quiet ourselves long enough, we might hear our child whisper, "Mommy, may I come out now?"

And after God has wiped away every tear, soothed your anguished heart, and comforted your grieving soul, you just may hear another voice: His voice, tender and loving, coaxing you with just one word. One name. *Yours.*

Each of us has a story to tell. In this sinful world, we are all at risk of becoming victims and, consequently, victimizers. The fallout from our poor choices, whether made in ignorance, selfishness, or deliberate malice, is always painful, wounding both ourselves and others. The hurts may surface right away or not for another twenty-five years—but they will surface one day. And when they do, you'll have a choice to make: will you turn and walk away, or will you reach out, seize God's hand, and face them together?

When I reached out to God, I never imagined where the

journey would lead. But this much I do know: one day, I will see my daughter again in Heaven. She will no longer be nameless and I will no longer be afraid. I will gather her in my arms, peer into her eyes, and tenderly whisper one word, one name, hers: "Amanda," which means *Worthy of Love.*

And so, dear reader, are you.

---

[1] Quoted from the book of Matthew, 1:20-21, NLT

[2] Quoted from the book of Luke, 23:34, NLT

Reflection Questions

VIII. The Gift

You, dear Sister, are worthy of love. When a child of God is tempted to question that truth, she doubts God's love, goodness, and faithfulness—*she doubts God!* His love for you is not based on anything you've done or haven't done but on God's own character. He loves you because He made you and He made you in order to love you—it's that simple.

Approximately 2,000 years ago, God chose to enter our world as a human being. Not as an adult, or a newborn, or even a fetus (which in Latin simply means, "little one") but as a fertilized egg. He didn't cut corners. He experienced all of the beginning stages of life, just as we do.

"Joseph son of David, do not be afraid to take Mary home as your wife, because what is conceived in her is from the Holy Spirit." (Matthew 1:20)

1. What thoughts come to mind as you consider this?

Review the following Scriptures:

God said, "...your wife Sarah will bear you a son, and you will call him Isaac." (Genesis 17:19)

The angel of the Lord also said to her: "You are now pregnant and you will give birth to a son. You shall name him Ishmael..." (Genesis 16:11)

But the angel said to him: "Do not be afraid, Zechariah; your prayer has been heard. Your wife Elizabeth will bear you a son, and you are to call him John."
(Luke 1:13)

[angel speaks to Joseph in a dream], "She will give birth to a son, and you are to give him the name Jesus, because he will save his people from their sins." (Matthew 1:21)

2. For each of the above verses, answer the following two questions in the space provided.

   a. What did God name the child?

   b. When did God name the child: before or after the child was born?

Verse	*Child's Name*	*Named Before or After Birth?*
Genesis 17:19		
Genesis 16:11		
Luke 1:13		
Matthew 1:21		

3. Read the following Scriptures slowly and out loud and then record your thoughts.

   a. "The Lord called me before my birth; from within the womb he called me by name."
      (Isaiah 49:1 NLT)

   b. "Before I formed you in the womb I knew you..."
      (Jeremiah 1: 5)

God makes no distinction of personhood between pre-born and born children. As a matter of fact, Jeremiah 1:5 says God knew us even before we were conceived!

According to Genesis 1:27, *"God created man[kind] in his own image, in the image of God he created him; male and female he created them."*

4. Based on these verses and all that you have learned so far, meditate on some of the inherent virtues all human beings possess from the moment God created each of them.

    a. On the next page is a blank table. In the first column, list as many virtues you can think of which all humans possess the moment they are created.

    b. As you consider each virtue, in the second and third columns, share some reflections about yourself and the child you lost.

    Below is an excerpt of my own table as an example. (feel free to use these to help you get started)

Virtue	Reflections about myself	Reflections about my child
Created in God's image	I am both body and spirit	Her spirit lives in Heaven
Worthy of protection	Thankful my parents chose life	She deserved to be protected
Worthy of love	Reject the lie: I am unlovable	God loves her; I can choose to love her, too.

Worthy of Love

Virtue	Reflections about myself

Reflections about my child

Jesus says, "It is Finished."

1 Peter 2:24 promises, *"He himself bore our sins in his body on the cross, so that we might die to sins and live for righteousness; by his wounds you have been healed."*

As the last drop of payment for sin fell to the ground, Jesus declared, "It is finished." In the Greek language, *it is finished* is actually one word "tetelestai" which is expressed in the perfect tense. This means that the meaning of the word refers to more than a one-time past event; the word also involves a present reality as well as a future consummation.

When we accept Jesus's payment for our sin, we are made holy and perfect in God's eyes from that very moment and for all eternity and yet, we remain in our sinful bodies in an unholy world as we await the glorious consummation of our souls.

Just as choosing to receive Jesus as our personal Lord and Savior is both a one-time event (when our salvation is secured forever) and a process (as we seek to cooperate with the Holy Spirit daily), we must also choose to receive His healing.

"...by his wounds you have been healed."

The word *healed* above is also in the Greek perfect tense. Healing is both a one-time event that occurs in the past (when we accept Jesus' death as payment for our sin, God declares us "healed") as well as a gift we must choose to live out daily by faith.

Believing what God says is true about you is a *choice*. But even if you choose to deny it, the truth of God's Word still stands.

5. In Chapter 4, you studied several truths about how God sees you. Go back and review pages 74-76.

What does God's Word declare about you?

 a. Are you struggling with any of these truths?
    Confess your unbelief and ask your heavenly
    Father for the faith to trust His Word. Write your
    prayer below.

*F*ather,

6. The next page lists additional changes that occur
   when a person receives Jesus as Lord and Savior
   by faith. Look up each verse and then complete the
   sentence using the key words.

Key Words

God's children

For you have been _____, not of perishable seed, but of imperishable, through the living and enduring word of God. (1 Peter 1:23)

Redeemed

Don't you know that you yourselves are _____ and that God's Spirit lives in you? (1 Corinthians 3:16)

Sanctified

...the Spirit you received brought about your _____ to sonship. And by him we cry, "Abba, Father." (Romans 8:15)

Eternal life

...rejoice that your _____ are written in heaven. (Luke 10:20)

Adoption

...But you were washed, you were _____, you were justified in the name of the Lord Jesus Christ and by the Spirit of our God. (1 Corinthians 6:11)

Names

I give them _____, and they shall never perish; no one will snatch them out of my hand. (John 10:28)

Born again

Therefore, since we have been _____ through faith, we have peace with God through our Lord Jesus Christ. (Romans 5:1)

Justified

Christ _____ us from the curse of the law by becoming a curse for us, for it is written: "Cursed is everyone who is hung on a tree. (Galatians 3:13)

God's Temple

The Spirit himself testifies with our spirit that we are _____. (Romans 8:16)

7. In light of all of these truths, answer the following two questions:

   a. Can both shame and peace exist together in the life of a believer? Why or why not?

   b. Should one who has been forgiven by God continue to punish herself with guilt over sin for which she has already confessed and repented? Why or why not?

Dear daughter of the King, when we, as children loved and forgiven by God, choose to walk in our old ways of sin, death, shame, and guilt, we bring disgrace to the gospel of Jesus Christ.

8. Through faith in Jesus Christ, we can **choose** to live differently, starting today. Review each verse below describing what God offers. Spend some time in prayer before completing the sentences that follow.

How much more, then, will the blood of Christ, who through the eternal Spirit offered himself unblemished to God, cleanse our consciences from acts that lead to death, so that we may serve the living God!

-Hebrews 9:14

I choose today to allow God to . . .

Peace I leave with you; my peace I give you. I do not give to you as the world gives. Do not let your hearts be troubled and do not be afraid.

-John 14:27

I choose today to receive . . .

We were therefore buried with him through baptism into death in order that, just as Christ was raised from the dead through the glory of the Father, we too may live a new life.

-Romans 6:4

I choose today . . .

Romans 6:4 reminds us that because of Christ, we each have an opportunity to choose to "live a new life." Today can mark a new beginning.

Perhaps you've spent years trying to forget, but now is the time to remember. Although none of us can give back life to our lost children, we can express our love and honor their memory by giving them a name.

When I first began looking at baby names, it started out as a mental exercise; only after God revealed how I had left my child nameless for twenty-five years, did the grief begin to surface. By God's grace I am healed today and as a result, I have named my daughter Amanda, which means "Worthy of Love."

Her name serves as a reminder that she, as well as you, me, and every person ever created, is worthy of love. Why? Because we were made by the hands of a loving Creator.

9. If you haven't decided on a name for your child, now may be the perfect time to do so. Spend some time in prayer and ask God to give you courage and insight in choosing a name for your child. If He chooses to provide it for you today, write it here:

   (If you find that you still need more time, I encourage you to commit the matter to prayer over the next week. Then return to this page and write what God has laid on your heart.)

10. Commemorate this day by honoring the memory of your child. If you are doing this study as a group, consider a way you can perform this "remembrance" together. Below are some ideas or you can choose one of your own:

    a. Write a letter or poem to your child.

    b. Write the name of your child on a balloon (or perhaps attach a note) and release it toward Heaven as a promise to be reunited.

    c. Visit a physical or online memorial site for children lost to abortion (such as www.abortionmemorial.com).

    d. Buy a pair of baby shoes and make them into a Christmas ornament to acknowledge your child's place in your family.

I am so proud of you! Below is a prayer I wish to pray over you:

Lord, bless your daughter who faithfully walked this difficult journey, who trusted you would be there with her and you proved Faithful. Now Lord, empower her to walk in newness of life by your Spirit, strengthen her by the knowledge of Jesus, the Word of Truth, and remind her she is the beloved daughter of the King and that you will never leave her or forsake her.

I'd love to hear how you or your group was impacted by this study or the unique way you chose to honor the memory of your child. Please contact me by visiting www.shadiahrichi.com.

Bless you, dear daughter of the King!

Shadia

A Mother's Hope
by Shadia Hrichi

Ungodly judges give birth to lies,
   with the pound of their gavel, babes have no name;
   with the stroke of a pen, children are banished to the grave.
In every city, the godless plot evil;
on every corner, they set their traps—
   lurking in darkness for the daughters of men.

They sacrifice children to the god of mammon;
   for an ounce of silver, innocent are slain,
   for a pound, a generation is forgotten.
Though her mother forsake her,
and the world has no room for her;
   Your arms receive her, and you call her daughter.

Within my heart a silent echo beats,
whispers taunt my soul;
   but my soul cannot hear,
   my heart cannot perceive
     what lays captive in the darkness.
I cannot bear the deafening silence! Tell me! Who is there?
   Can a mother mourn for the forgotten?
   Can a memorial carve a place for the nameless?

Then you opened my eyes to understanding—
   you have not abandoned her to the grave.
You heard my cry and answered me,
   "Give your child a name."

Before you formed her in the womb,
angels announced her arrival;
    When your heart conceived her,
    heaven burst into song: "Worthy of Love!"

My Lord, my Redeemer!
    With pounded nails, you deliver me from the grave;
    by your blood, my transgression is blotted out;
        you rise, and call me daughter.

Four things I do not understand—
five are too wonderful for me:
    You have taught my soul a lullaby,
    and filled my arms with laughter;
    my tears have become a song,
    and my silence a beautiful voice—
        you have turned my secret into a stage.

I will praise your Name to the congregation!
    To the nations I will lift my voice!
        May all the peoples of the earth glorify your name!

Stay Connected

• Be among the first to hear about Shadia's next book
• Learn of exclusive discounts and book giveaways
• Find out where Shadia is speaking next

Visit *shadiahrichi.com* to subscribe for updates

Follow on Social Media

Follow Shadia on your favorite social media sites,
including FaceBook, Pinterest, GoodReads, YouTube,
Twitter, Instgram, and LinkedIn

Start a Group

Leader's Guide and other resources available at
www.shadiahrichi.com

Questions/Comments?

Send an email to info@shadiahrichi.com

MORE FROM

Shadia Hrichi

Don't miss these fascinating studies in Shadia's new "Behind the Seen" series:

Discover a close relationship with God—no matter the pain or suffering in your life. Witness the depths of God's compassion through the eyes of Hagar, a runaway slave who meets the living God in a desert of despair and gives Him the name, "The God Who Sees Me."

(HAGAR: Rediscovering the God Who Sees Me is a 7-week, in-depth Bible study)

"Deep and packed with surprising insights!"
-FRANCINE RIVERS

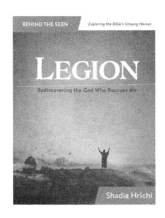

Experience God's relentless love through the eyes of a tormented cutter as you step into the fascinating story of the man known only by the name of the demons that haunted him. Climb into the boat with Jesus as He heads into enemy territory where He battles violent storms and armies of demons in order to rescue . . . *one . . . lost . . . soul.*

(LEGION: Rediscovering the God Who Rescues Me is a 6-week, in-depth Bible study)

Stay up-to-date on Shadia's books and speaking events with her *free* eNewsletter. Sign up today at *shadiahrichi.com.*

Leader's Guide:
Introduction

May the Lord richly bless you for your desire to lead a *Worthy of Love* study group. Because God is sovereign, nothing happens by chance. You are reading this right now by His own design. May the Lord bless you and guide as you prepare to come alongside women whom God has made ready to walk this tender journey.

Following this introduction are some practical guidelines to consider before you plan your first group. However, even before you ponder any instructions, the single most important preparation is to surrender your heart to the work the Holy Spirit has called you to. One of the best ways to do this is by endeavoring to understand, to the best of your ability, the specific heartbreak and trauma suffered by women who have lost children to abortion.

Even if you have not personally had an abortion, if you are going to be used as God's instrument of healing in such a tender ministry, it is imperative that you first prepare your mind, heart, and soul to come alongside the women whom you will serve by prayerfully going through this study on your own. While you may not be able to answer every question, each lesson centers on a key principle taken directly from God's Word. Chapters include:

1. *The Lie*: REPLACING THE LIES WITH GOD'S TRUTH

2. *The Secret*: EXPOSING OUR SECRETS TO GOD'S LIGHT

3. *The Crossroads*: STANDING AT THE CROSSROADS OF GOD'S LOVE

4. *The Mask*: EMBRACING OUR TRUE IDENTITY IN CHRIST

5. *The Stone*: SURRENDERING OUR BURDENS TO GOD

6. *The Battle*: Confronting Our Giants with God's Word

7. *The Wish*: Entrusting Our Hearts to The Healer

8. *The Gift*: Choosing to Receive God's Promises

The timeless truths of God's Word are the sole source of everlasting hope, healing, love, and forgiveness each of our hearts is longing for - and these are available to us only through the victory won by our glorious Lord and Savior Jesus Christ.

Please know you are in my prayers. Truly, the Lord has great things in store for you as you serve Him by ministering to His precious daughters. To Him alone be all the glory!

> *"Blessed be the God and Father of our Lord Jesus Christ, the Father of mercies and God of all comfort, who comforts us in all our affliction, so that we may be able to comfort those who are in any affliction, with the comfort with which we ourselves are comforted by God."*
> (2 Corinthians 1:3-4 ESV)

Shadia

Leader's Guide
Table of Contents

Worthy of Love

Leader's Guide:
General Instructions

This Leader's Guide was created to offer a suggested framework and practical tips as you lead your group. To make it easy for you to guide participants through the study, except for the Leader's Guide and an updated "Acknowledgements" page, this book is identical to the participant's version of *Worthy of Love.*

While most groups are conducted using an 8-week format, some groups have used a modified 4.5-week format. Both versions are included in this Guide.

Depending on the size of your group, review of each chapter should take approximately one and one-half hours; nevertheless, it is recommended that you schedule two hours each week for flexibility. Group sizes vary and typically include three to eight participants.

It is not necessary that the group leader has experienced losing a child to abortion. However, if you desire to lead a group but have not personally lost a child to abortion, please be sure to invite a co-leader or helper who is post-abortive to serve alongside you. This will provide the women with a sense of comfort and connection. Each leader and co-leader (whether post-abortive or not) should personally work through the book prior to committing to serve a group.

If you are conducting the group in a host home, invite the host to serve as a helper. The greatest gift each of us brings to the women God entrusts to our care is our support, love, and encouragement - and for these, there is no prerequisite. Also, leaders and helpers who are not post-abortive should still work through the homework for each chapter. Not every question will be applicable, of course, but there are many Scripture assignments that are applicable to all of us. Encourage their participation in these areas. This will further help the group (including leaders and helpers) to bond.

For each session, key discussion questions are provided for each chapter's homework. If there is still time remaining, you may opt to review the questions that were skipped. In some instances, I've also included suggested sharing time allotments for certain questions. These should be adjusted depending on the size and make-up of your group and of course, the leading of the Holy Spirit.

Please remain mindful that some women in the group may have had more than one abortion. As you present each question, be sure to leave room for women to process each loss separately.

You may encounter a time when you feel a participant could benefit from professional counseling. I recommend that before beginning a study, you identify one or two local Christian counselors to whom you can refer. Most are willing to engage in an informal phone conversation where you can inquire about their experience in counseling post-abortive women. Some may even be willing to offer a discounted rate. Feel free to ask the counselor about her views on abortion and on a woman's need for healing after abortion.

You may like the idea of beginning each session by playing a worship song. I've included some suggestions at the beginning of each session.

At the end of this guide, I have included a variety of forms, poems, and other documents to enrich your group experience and to help prepare you and the participants for the journey ahead. These are provided for your convenience and may be utilized at your sole discretion. Not every group uses all of the forms so feel free to pick and choose what works best for you.

Above all, may the Holy Spirit lead you as you serve Him. Truly, I am honored to partner with you in this ministry. I am excited for all God has in mind to do in you and through you!

To Him alone be all the glory. Amen!

Before You Begin

A few items to consider as you plan your group

PARTNERING WITH YOUR CHURCH
Take some time to meet and talk with your pastor or women's ministry leader to share your passion and vision for the ministry. Provide him or her with a copy of the book to review.

LOCATION
Prayfully choose a location. Although it is not necessary, many groups are hosted in private homes where the atmosphere can be relaxed. If the group will be taking place at a church, choose a location away from other activities. Whatever location you choose, keep the details confidential and only share it with the group members (and other key supporters, such as church leadership).

PROMOTION
To assist in spreading awareness of the study at your church, in your community, and on social media, the following free resources are available at www.shadiahrichi.com:

- Church bulletin inserts (PDF download)
- Flyers/Posters (PDF download)
- Promo video (video link)

SCHOLARSHIPS
Consider having a scholarship available to help cover the cost of books.

PRAYER SUPPORT

Enlist a network of prayer supporter to bathe you, your co-leaders/ helpers/hosts, and the women God will entrust to your care, in prayer.

What to Bring

Suggestions on what to bring for ALL sessions

- Your copy of *Worthy of Love* (plus extra copy in case someone needs one)
- Music
- Pens
- Bible (consider bringing an extra Bible in case someone needs one)
- Name Badges
- Tissues
- Snacks (suggestion: always have chocolate on hand :)
- Water
- Blank Prayer Cards

Additional items you will need
(session numbers based on 8-week format)

Session 1
- Books for each participant
- Copies of the following forms:
  - Group Etiquette
  - Commitment form
  - Confidentiality Waiver
  - Sign up/Contact Information

Session 4
- Copies of "Before Me, You" poem

Session 7
- Attractive Blank Note Cards for each participant to take home for exercise on page 158

Session 8

- Copies of poem "A Pre-born Child's Conversation With His Heavenly Father" by Delia Baker Hutto March
- Candles (one candle for each child lost, including children of leaders/co-leaders/helpers, plus extra candle to light all the others)
- Suggested: small gift for each participant

Note: All forms, documents, and poems referenced in this Leader's Guide are included at the end of this Guide and are available for free download at www.shadiahrichi.com

(Session One)
Welcome

BEFORE THE SESSION
- Read "A Note from the Author." Underline key phrases to discuss
- Read "Foreword by Brian Fisher" and the poem "A Mother's Lament." Note anything that you wish to share with the group
- Be prepared to introduce yourself and what you hope to gain from your time together
- Schedule time prior to the start of the session for leader, co-leader, and host to pray together
- Review "What to Bring" on pages 173-174

WELCOME
- Welcome the group. Commend them for participating and for making the time to care for themselves when so many other things compete for their time
- Opening prayer

INTRODUCTIONS (2-3 minutes each)
- Introduce yourself and share what led you to serve as leader/co-leader
- Ask each person (including co-leaders) to introduce herself, including her name and what she hopes to gain from the study
- Optional: Distribute and review "Objectives of the **Worthy of Love** study group"

REVIEW FORMS
- Distribute and review "Group Etiquette" form
- Review and ask participants to read and sign "Commitment form"
- Distribute and review "Confidentiality waiver"
- Ask participants provide their name and contact information on the sign up form

DISTRIBUTE BOOKS
- Distribute books
- Read aloud (or invite participants to read silently) "A Note from the Author" and to share their thoughts

- Optional: Read aloud (or invite participants to read silently) "Foreword by Brian Fisher" and to share their thoughts
- Optional: Invite participants to read "A Mother's Lament." Ask participants what stood out to them in the poem

REMINDERS & CLOSING

- Present blank Prayer Cards and encourage participants to share their prayer requests (prayer cards to be collected at end of each sessions for leader/co-leader to pray over)
- Advise participants of the importance of carving out time to do the homework each week in order to listen for God's leading. Be mindful that the enemy does not want them to be healed; they are likely to encounter spiritual warfare and distractions along the way
- Closing prayer (pray for participants' prayer requests and for them to sense God's Peace and Presence and as they work through the study)
- Remind participants to complete the homework in Chapter One for the next session

NOTES

(Session Two)
Chapter One: "The Lie"
Replacing the Lies with God's Truth

BEFORE THE SESSION
- Read chapter One "The Lie"
- Review discussion questions
- Email a note of encouragement to the participants
- Select a worship song to share (suggestion: In His Time by Maranatha Music)
- Select a Scripture to share (suggestion: *"The Lord himself goes before you and will be with you; he will never leave you nor forsake you."* (Deuteronomy 31:8 NIV)
- Review "What to Bring" on pages 173-174

WELCOME
- Welcome the group
- Ask if anyone brought a worship song to share (optional)
- Play worship song (optional)
- Set the tone with Scripture
- Opening prayer

OVERVIEW
(Consider reading or re-stating in your own words)
Every choice we make effects how we view our self, the world, and even God. While abortion may provide a temporary relief from stress and fear, in the long run, instead of bringing freedom, abortion often leaves us in captivity. In this session, we will explore the lies we believed and examine them in light of God's Truth.

SHARING OUR STORIES (2-3 min. ea.)
Take turns answering the following questions (*Note: leaders/co-leaders who are post-abortive should share first*)
- How many abortions have you had and do you recall how old were you each time?

- If you remember how far along you were in each pregnancy, what did you believe about your pregnancy in terms of fetal development?

HOMEWORK
What Abortion Did to Me
- Introduce question 1 on page 6; share a personal example (or review author's examples)
- Discuss responses/fill-ins on pages 6-7

Lies about Pregnancy
- Depending on the group's comfort level, invite participants to take turns reading each lie and the Scripture verses on page 11 or the leader and co-leader can read them
- Discuss question 6 on page 12
- Discuss question 9 on page 14

Lies about God
- Invite participants to take turns reading each lie and the Scripture verses on page 15
- Ask participants which Scripture captured their attention the most? Why?
- Discuss responses to question 15

Lies about Myself
- Invite participants to take turns reading each lie and the Scripture verses on page 18
- Discuss question 17 on page 19
- (Optional) Re-read the first paragraph at the bottom of page 20
- Discuss questions 19 through 21

IF TIME REMAINS
- Ask participants if they wish to discuss any questions that were skipped
- Review "Lesson Summary" at the end of the chapter
- Invite participants to discuss any other highlights from the homework they'd like to share

REMINDERS

- Next week's homework: Chapter Two
- Attendance: Importance of attending all sessions
- Time: Everyone's time is valuable; importance of arriving on time
- Songs: Invite participants to bring a song to share next time
- Prayer: Remind participants to turn in prayer cards, if desired

CLOSING

- Play closing song (optional)
- Closing Prayer

NOTES

(Session Three)
Chapter Two: "The Secret"
Exposing Our Secrets To God's Light

BEFORE THE SESSION
- Read chapter Two "The Secret"
- Review discussion questions
- Email a note of encouragement to the participants
- Select a worship song to share (suggestion: East to West by Casting Crowns)
- Select a Scripture to share (suggestion: *"But God demonstrates his own love for us in this: While we were still sinners, Christ died for us."* Romans 5:8)
- Review "What to Bring" on pages 173-174

WELCOME
- Welcome the group
- Ask if anyone brought a worship song to share (optional)
- Play worship song (optional)
- Set the tone with Scripture
- Opening prayer

OVERVIEW
(Consider reading or re-stating in your own words)
Keeping secrets invariably leads us to hide from one another and from God. Because God is holy, these internalized secrets create a barrier between God and us. Over time, we may come to believe (either consciously or subconsciously) that God cannot forgive us, or use us, or love us.

SHARING OUR STORIES (2-3 min. ea.)
Take turns answering the following questions (*Suggestion: Leaders/co-leaders who are post-abortive should share first*)
   - Who went with you when you underwent the abortion(s)?
   - What stands out the most in your memory about the abortion facility or your experience?
   - After the abortion(s), did you tell anyone else?

HOMEWORK

- Discuss questions 1-2 on pages 29-30
- Read paragraph on page 30 and introduce question 3
- Discuss question 3 on pages 30-31
- Read or briefly summarize 1 Samuel 16 on page 32. For example, you might say something like, *King David was likely an adolescent when God chose him to be king over Israel; however, David would not become king until many years later*
- Read or invite participants to read text beginning at the bottom of page 32 ("in the spring of the year….") through all of page 33
- Discuss questions 4 – 6 on page 34 (Reading of 10 Commandments is optional)
- Read Scripture verse on page 36
- Discuss questions 9-10 on pages 36-37
- Read Scriptures on page 38
- Discuss questions 11-12 on pages 38-39
- Read or briefly summarize Exodus 3-4 on pages 39-40. For example, you might say, *God appears to Moses and tells him to confront Pharaoh, demanding that he let God's people go, but Moses makes excuses and eventually asks God "please send someone else"*
- Discuss question 16 on page 41
- Read both paragraphs at bottom of page 43
- Discuss Lesson Summary on page 45

IF TIME REMAINS

- Ask participants if they wish to discuss any questions that were skipped
- Review "Lesson Summary" at the end of the chapter
- Invite participants to discuss any other highlights from the homework they'd like to share

REMINDERS

- Next week's homework: Chapter Three
- Attendance: Importance of attending all sessions
- Time: Everyone's time is valuable; importance of arriving on time
- Songs: Invite participants to bring a song to share next time
- Prayer: Remind participants to turn in prayer cards, if desired

CLOSING
- Play closing song (optional)
- Closing Prayer

NOTES

(Session Four)
Chapter Three: "The Crossroads"
Standing at the Crossroads
of God's Love

BEFORE THE SESSION
- Read chapter Three "The Crossroads"
- Review discussion questions
- Email a note of encouragement to the participants
- Select a worship song to share (suggestion: How Deep the Father's Love for Us by Phillips, Craig & Dean)
- Select a Scripture to share (suggestion: *"'For I know the plans I have for you,' declares the Lord, 'plans to prosper you and not to harm you, plans to give you hope and a future.'"* Jeremiah 29:11)
- Review "What to Bring" on pages 173-174
- Optional: bring copies of poem "Before Me, You"

WELCOME
- Welcome the group
- Ask if anyone brought a worship song to share (optional)
- Play worship song (optional)
- Set the tone with Scripture
- Opening prayer

OVERVIEW
Abortion is a traumatic experience; however, every woman processes trauma differently. Grief can manifest itself in many ways but no matter where we are, God is willing to meet us there. It is at the Crossroads, where our grief intersects with God's forgiveness, where healing begins.

SHARING OUR STORIES (2-3 min. ea.)
Take turns answering the following questions
- How long ago was the abortion(s)?
- What kind of emotions (if any) did you experience afterwards?
- Did your feelings change over time? If so, how?

HOMEWORK
- Discuss question 1-2 on page 51-53
- Read 2 Timothy 1:9-10 on page 53
- Discuss questions 3-5 on page 54-56
- Review fill-in answers for question 6 on pages 58-59 (consider inviting participants to take turns reading)
- Invite group (including leader/co-leader/helper) to discuss/share their answers to the following questions:

  o Which truth in question 6 do you struggle to believe and why?
  o Which truth in question 6 was most meaningful to you and why?

GOSPEL *(pages 60-61)*
Acknowledge that someone in the group may have accepted God's offer of salvation for the first time. Invite anyone who made a decision to follow Jesus to share their decision either with the group or, if she prefers, privately with you (or the co-leader) afterwards.

OPTIONAL
Distribute copies of the poem "Before Me, You." Consider having someone read it out loud. Invite the group to share their thoughts.

REMINDERS
- Next week's homework: Chapter Four
- Attendance: Importance of attending all sessions
- Time: Everyone's time is valuable; importance of arriving on time
- Songs: Invite participants to bring a song to share next time
- Prayer: Remind participants to turn in prayer cards, if desired

CLOSING
- Play closing song (optional)
- Closing Prayer

NOTES

(Session Five)
Chapter Four: "The Mask"
Embracing our True Identity in Christ

BEFORE THE SESSION
- Read chapter Four "The Mask"
- Review discussion questions
- Email a note of encouragement to the participants
- Select a worship song to share (suggestion: Remind Me Who I Am by Jason Gray)
- Select a Scripture to share (suggested: *"The Lord does not look at the things people look at. People look at the outward appearance, but the Lord looks at the heart."* -1 Samuel 16:7 NIV)
- Review "What to Bring" on pages 173-174

WELCOME
- Welcome the group
- Ask if anyone brought a worship song to share (optional)
- Play worship song (optional)
- Set the tone with Scripture
- Opening prayer

OVERVIEW
Buried secrets are fertile ground for Satan to plant accusations in our minds and hearts. These accusations, if not surrendered to God's Truth, will eventually transform into self-condemnation, leading us further away from what God says is true about us.

OPTIONAL
Ask the group:
- What comes to your mind when you think of someone who wears a mask?
- What are some reasons people might hide behind a mask?

SHARING OUR STORIES (2-3 min. ea.)
Take turns answering the following questions, which are on pages 67-68 (questions 2-3):

> o Do you believe you have suppressed your feelings about having an abortion? If so, how?
> o Do you have a mask? If so, how would you describe it?

HOMEWORK
- Read Jeremiah 17:9 on the top of page 69
- Discuss questions 4-7 (if you are short on time, focus on questions 5 and 7)
- Ask participants to read silently along with you as you read aloud the bottom of page 72 and all of page 73
- Discuss what they just read on pages 72-73
- Participants to take turns reading Scripture verses on pages 74 and 76; after each Scripture ask the group to share what Keywords they chose (questions 8-9, note some key words may work for more than one Scripture)
- Discuss question 10 (which refers readers back to pages 70-71)
- If there is time, discuss question 11, otherwise skip to question 13 on page 78
- Ask if anyone wishes to share from questions 13-14 on pages 78-79

IF TIME REMAINS
- Ask participants if they wish to discuss any questions that were skipped
- Review "Lesson Summary" at the end of the chapter
- Invite participants to discuss any other highlights from the homework they would like to share

REMINDERS
- Next week's homework: Chapter Five
- Attendance: Importance of attending all sessions
- Time: Everyone's time is valuable; importance of arriving on time
- Songs: Invite participants to bring a song to share next time
- Prayer: Remind participants to turn in prayer cards, if desired

CLOSING
- Play closing song (optional)
- Closing Prayer

Worthy of Love

NOTES

(Session Six)
Chapter Five: "The Stone"
Surrendering our Burdens to God

BEFORE THE SESSION
- Read chapter Five "The Stone"
- Review discussion questions
- Email a note of encouragement to the participants
- Select a worship song to share (suggestion: At the Foot of the Cross by Women of Faith)
- Select a Scripture to share (suggested: *"Come to me, all you who are weary and burdened, and I will give you rest."* - Matthew 11:28 NIV)
- Review "What to Bring" on pages 173-174

WELCOME
- Welcome the group
- Ask if anyone brought a worship song to share (optional)
- Play worship song (optional)
- Set the tone with Scripture
- Opening prayer

OVERVIEW
The burdens we carry will look different for each one of us: the fears, regrets, guilt, emotional numbness, or shame we had been punishing ourselves with as a result of our choices. God knows they are too heavy for us; that is why He wants us to surrender them to Him.

SHARING OUR STORIES (2-3 min. ea.)
Take turns answering the following questions, which are on pages 88-89 (questions 1-3):
- How long ago was the abortion (or abortions)?
- Do you believe the saying "time heals all wounds?" Why or why not?
- Is this the first step you have taken toward healing? What has, or has not, been helpful up to this point?

HOMEWORK
- Ask the group if there is anything they would like to share from question 6 on pages 91-93
- Discuss question 7 on page 94
- Discuss question 9-10 on page 96
  - If you answered yes to question 10, did you try the suggestion to pray for the person you struggle to forgive? What were the results?
- Encourage each participant to share their acronyms and/or drawings on pages 98-99

IF TIME REMAINS
- Ask participants if they wish to discuss any questions that were skipped
- Review "Lesson Summary" at the end of the chapter
- Invite participants to discuss any other highlights from the homework they'd like to share

REMINDERS
- Next week's homework: Chapter Six
- Attendance: Importance of attending all sessions
- Time: Everyone's time is valuable; importance of arriving on time
- Songs: Invite participants to bring a song to share next time
- Prayer: Remind participants to turn in prayer cards, if desired

CLOSING
- Play closing song (optional)
- Closing Prayer

NOTES

(Session Seven)
Chapter Six: "The Battle"
Confronting our Giants with
The Word of God

BEFORE THE SESSION
- Read chapter Six "The Battle"
- Review discussion questions
- What to bring: attractive stationary with envelopes for each participant to take home. They will use the stationary to complete exercise 10a on page 158 for the last session. Suggestion: using a sticky note, write a brief note or prayer and place inside each envelope; however, ask participants not to jump ahead or open the envelopes until they reach page 158
- Email a note of encouragement to the participants
- Select a worship song to share (suggestion: A Mighty Fortress by Christy Nockels)
- Select a Scripture to share (suggested: Ephesians 6:10-17)
- Review "What to Bring" on pages 173-174

WELCOME
- Welcome the group
- Ask if anyone brought a worship song to share (optional)
- Play worship song (optional)
- Set the tone with Scripture
- Opening prayer

OVERVIEW
As we walk through our journeys, we have discovered how lies inevitably require us to keep secrets. In order to keep the secrets, we must hide behind a mask. All of this deception burdens our souls with weights too heavy for us to carry. Even after we surrender our burdens to God, battles can still rage in our minds and in our hearts. There is only one weapon powerful enough to crush the schemes of the enemy warring against us: the Word of God.

"We destroy arguments and every lofty opinion raised against the knowledge of God, and take every thought captive to obey Christ..." (2 Corinthians 10:5).

SHARING OUR STORIES (2-3 min. ea.)

Take turns answering the following questions, which are on page 112 (question 3-4):

- o After the abortion, did you sense a change in your relationship with God? If so, how?
- o After the abortion, did you sense a change in your relationship with others? If so, how?

HOMEWORK

- Ask participants if there is anything they want to share from pages 108-111
- Discuss question 2 on page 111
- Discuss question 5 on page 113
- Ask participants if there is anything they want to share from pages 115-116
- Discuss question 8-9 on page 118-119
- Ask participants if there is anything they want to share from pages 121-122
- Take turns sharing what each person found most significant from the week's lesson ("Lesson Summary" on page 123) and why it was meaningful to them

IF TIME REMAINS

- Ask participants if they wish to discuss any questions that were skipped
- Review "Lesson Summary" at the end of the chapter
- Invite participants to discuss any other highlights from the homework they'd like to share

REMINDERS

- *IMPORTANT*: next week's homework includes Chapters Seven AND Eight
- Give each participant one of the pretty blank notecards in an unsealed envelope; explain they are not to open it until they reach the exercise on page 158

CLOSING
- Play closing song (optional)
- Closing Prayer

NOTES

(Session Eight)
Chapters Seven & Eight

"Our Wish" & "His Gift"
Releasing the Memories of Our Children

BEFORE THE SESSION

- Read chapter Seven "The Wish" and Eight "The Gift"
- Review discussion questions
- Review "What to Bring" on pages 173-174
- IMPORTANT: Prepare for the "Ceremony of Remembrance"
    - Email a note of encouragement to the participants; remind them to complete exercise 10a on page 158 and to bring their notes to the last session
    - Read question 10 on page 158 for a list of ideas to incorporate into your ceremony
    - Leaders/co-leaders/helpers who are post-abortive should also complete exercise 10a and be prepared to share their letters with the group
    - Choose a song to play in the background during the ceremony (suggested: instrumental worship song playing softly and continuously in a loop; suggestion: *How Deep the Father's Love for Us - Instrumental*)
    - Bring copies of "Heavenly Conversation" poem
    - Bring candles (one candle for each child lost, including the children of leaders/co-leaders/helpers that were lost to abortion, plus extra 'torch' candle to light all the others)
    - Suggested: small gift for each participant (such as a white rose)
    - Bring copies of "Evaluation" form
- Select a worship song to share at beginning of session (suggestion: Amazing Grace)
- Select a Scripture to share (suggested: *"Daughter, your faith has healed you. Go in peace and be freed from your suffering."* – Mark 5:34 NIV)

WELCOME
- Welcome the group
- Play worship song (optional)
- Set the tone with Scripture
- Opening prayer

OVERVIEW
We always have a choice. God's Word never fails but we must choose to believe it. God's promises cannot be broken but we must choose to receive them. His Word says we are forgiven and He promises to heal us. 1 Peter 2:24 promises, *"He himself bore our sins in his body on the cross, so that we might die to sins and live for righteousness; 'by his wounds you have been healed.'"* (1 Peter 2:24 NIV)

HOMEWORK
Chapter 7 "The Wish"
- Discuss question 2 on page 130
- Discuss question 7 on page 133
- Discuss question 10 on page 136
- Discuss question 12-13 on page 138

Chapter 8 "The Gift"
- Discuss question 1 on page 146
- Ask if anyone has anything else they want to share from pages 150-151
- Discuss question 5 on pages 152-153
- Briefly review Keywords/Scriptures on page 154
- Ask if anyone has anything else they want to share from pages 156-157
- Ask if anyone read "A Mothers' Hope" on page 160 (optional)

MINI BREAK
(Set up for ceremony)

SETUP

- Prepare music (instrumental worship song to play softly in background in a continuous loop)
- Arrange unlit candles, including "torch" candle, which will be used to light the other candles
- Have gifts (such as roses) ready, but out of sight

CEREMONY OF REMEMBRANCE

- Begin music
- Give each participant a copy of "Heavenly Conversation" poem to read silently
- Take turns (including leaders/helpers) reading aloud the letters/poems written to each lost child (exercise 10a on page 158)
- Gather around the candles and pray a simple prayer for the group. A sample prayer might be, *"Father, we are here tonight to honor the memory of our children and to thank you that they are safe in Your arms. We look forward to one day being reunited with them in Heaven. Amen."*
- Using the the 'torch' candle, be the first to light a candle to honor the memory of your own child(ren) with simple words, such as *"I light this candle in honor of my daughter Amanda."* (If you have not personally lost a child to abortion, you may elect to light a candle for a family member you have lost to abortion or simply delegate this task to a co-leader or helper who is post-abortive).
- Pass the 'torch' candle to the next participant, who will follow your example. If someone has lost more than one child, she should light a candle for each of her children before passing the 'torch' candle to the next participant.
- Offer a closing prayer

CLOSING

- Ask participants to complete Evaluation form
- Encourage participants to help spread awareness of the study by sharing a review on Amazon.com or Christianbook.com or visiting the **Worthy of Love** Facebook or Pinterest page
- Collect evaluation forms
- Give each participant a parting gift

AFTER THE SESSION

- Contact participants in the days/weeks following to encourage them and offer your support if they are considering leading a **Worthy of Love** group of their own
- Participant and leader feedback is vital to the ongoing development and effectiveness of the ministry. Please send evaluation forms (see additional forms/helpful documents) to:

  o Email: info@shadiahrichi.com

  o Postal mail:

  Shadia Hrichi, Author/Speaker
  PO Box 24874
  San Jose, CA 95154

NOTES

Modified (4.5-Week) Schedule
Introduction

BENEFITS & CHALLENGES

This modified schedule provides some benefits as well as some challenges when compared to the typical 8-week format. It also requires some additional pre-planning, which is outlined below.

Benefits include being able to offer participants (and leaders) a shorter time commitment in terms of number of sessions (total hours invested is the same as in the 8-week format). The half-day retreat also provides a wonderful opportunity for women in the group to bond. Further, by the time participants have completed the first session, they will be substantially invested in their healing; therefore, they are far more likely to return and complete the remaining sessions.

Some challenges include making sure that participants have access to books several weeks prior to the first session in order for them to arrive prepared. In addition, participants will need to work through the first three chapters of the book on their own without the benefit of group support.

Despite the challenges, this format is well-suited for women who are motivated to complete the assignments and who find a shorter time commitment more appealing.

PLANNING & LOGISTICS

- This format includes one half-day mini-retreat followed by one evening each week for four weeks (sample schedule to follow)
- Because participants will need to complete the homework for chapters 1-3 prior to the first session, be prepared to offer instructions on how participants can obtain copies of the books
- It is recommended that registration/sign-up for the study closes approximately two weeks prior to the first session in order to give participants time to complete all of the homework for chapters 1-3
- Be prepared to serve a light lunch or brunch during the half-day retreat

Modified Schedule
Introduction

SCHEDULE

- Below is a suggested schedule (if the size of your group exceeds five participants, consider extending the half-day retreat by one hour)
- *Note: be sure to leave enough time between the half-day retreat and the next group meeting to allow participants to complete the homework for the next session. For example, if the half-day retreat is scheduled for Saturday and the remaining sessions will be held on Mondays, then skip the first Monday that follows the Saturday half-day retreat*

Session One: SATURDAY 9am – 1pm
Chapter One "The Lie"
Chapter Two "The Secret"
~ Break for Lunch ~
Chapter Three "The Crossroads"

Session Two: WEDNESDAY 7pm – 9pm
Chapter Four "The Mask"

Session Three: WEDNESDAY 7pm – 9pm
Chapter Five "The Stone"

Session Four: WEDNESDAY 7pm – 9pm
Chapter Six "The Battle"

Session Five: WEDNESDAY 7pm – 9pm
Chapter Seven & Eight "The Wish" & "The Gift"

(Session One)
Half-day Retreat

BEFORE THE SESSION

- Read "A Note from the Author." Underline key phrases to discuss
- Read "Foreword by Brian Fisher" and the poem "A Mother's Lament." Note anything that you wish to share with the group
- Read chapters One, Two and Three and review discussion questions
- Be prepared to introduce yourself and what you hope to gain from your time together
- Schedule time prior to the start of the session for leader, co-leader, and host to pray together
- Optional: bring copies of the following forms to review/complete at the first session:
  - Group Etiquette
  - Commitment Form
  - Confidentiality Waiver
- Select a Scripture to share (suggestion: *"The Lord himself goes before you and will be with you; he will never leave you nor forsake you."* - Deuteronomy 31:8 NIV)
- Select a worship song to share (suggestion: In His Time by Maranatha Music)
- Email a note of encouragement to the participants
- Optional: bring copies of the poem "Before Me, You" to give to each participant at the end of the half-day session
- Before you begin, review "What to Bring" on pages 173-174

Reminder: All forms, documents, and poems referenced in this Leader's Guide are included at the end of this Guide and are available for free download at www.shadiahrichi.com

INTRODUCTION
~ 15 minutes ~

WELCOME & INTRODUCTIONS
- Welcome the group. Commend them for participating and for making the time to care for themselves when so many other things compete for their time
- Introduce yourself and share what led you to serve as leader/co-leader
- Ask each person (including co-leaders) to introduce herself, including her name and what she hopes to gain from the study

REVIEW FORMS (Optional)
- Distribute and review "Group Etiquette" form
- Review and ask participants to read and sign "Commitment form"
- Distribute and review "Confidentiality waiver"

OPENING PRAYER
- Set the tone with Scripture
- Play a worship song
- Opening prayer

CHAPTER ONE: THE LIE
(taken from pages 177–178)
~ 1 hour ~

OVERVIEW
(Consider reading or re-stating in your own words)
Every choice we make effects how we view our self, the world, and even God. While abortion may provide a temporary relief from stress and fear, in the long run, instead of bringing freedom, abortion often leaves us in captivity. In this session, we will explore the lies we believed and examine them in light of God's Truth.

SHARING OUR STORIES (2-3 min. ea.)

Take turns answering the following questions (*Note: leaders/co-leaders who are post-abortive should share first*)

- How many abortions have you had and do you recall how old were you each time?
- If you remember how far along you were in each pregnancy, what did you believe about your pregnancy in terms of fetal development?

HOMEWORK

What Abortion Did to Me
- ○ Introduce question 1 on page 6; share a personal example (or review author's examples)
- ○ Discuss responses/fill-ins on pages 6-7

Lies about Pregnancy
- ○ Depending on the group's comfort level, invite participants to take turns reading each lie and the Scripture verses on page 11 or the leader and co-leader can read them
- ○ Discuss question 6 on page 12
- ○ Discuss question 9 on page 14

Lies about God
- ○ Invite participants to take turns reading each lie and the Scripture verses on page 15
- ○ Ask participants which Scripture captured their attention the most? Why?
- ○ Discuss responses to question 15

Lies about Myself
- ○ Invite participants to take turns reading each lie and the Scripture verses on page 18
- ○ Discuss question 17 on page 19
- ○ (Optional) Re-read the first paragraph at the bottom of page 20
- ○ Discuss questions 19 through 21

IF TIME REMAINS

- Ask participants if they wish to discuss any questions that were skipped

- Review "Lesson Summary" at the end of the chapter
- Invite participants to discuss any other highlights from the homework they'd like to share

NOTES

~ Mini Break (15 minutes) ~

CHAPTER TWO: THE SECRET
(taken from pages 180–181)
~ 1 hour ~

OVERVIEW
(Consider reading or re-stating in your own words)

Keeping secrets invariably leads us to hide from one another and from God. Because God is holy, these internalized secrets create a barrier between God and us. Over time, we may come to believe (either consciously or subconsciously) that God cannot forgive us, or use us, or love us.

SHARING OUR STORIES (2-3 min. ea.)

Take turns answering the following questions (*Suggestion: Leaders/co-leaders who are post-abortive should share first*)

- o Who went with you when you underwent the abortion(s)?
- o What stands out the most in your memory about the abortion facility or your experience?
- o After the abortion(s), did you tell anyone else?

HOMEWORK

- Discuss questions 1-2 on pages 29-30
- Read paragraph on page 30 and introduce question 3
- Discuss question 3 on pages 30-31
- Read or briefly summarize 1 Samuel 16 on page 32. For example, you might say something like, *King David was likely an adolescent when God chose him to be king over Israel; however, David would not become king until many years later*
- Read or invite participants to read text beginning at the bottom of page 32 ("in the spring of the year….") through all of page 33
- Discuss questions 4 – 6 on page 34 (Reading of 10 Commandments is optional)
- Read Scripture verse on page 36
- Discuss questions 9-10 on pages 36-37
- Read Scriptures on page 38
- Discuss questions 11-12 on pages 38-39
- Read or briefly summarize Exodus 3-4 on pages 39-40. For example, you might say, *God appears to Moses and tells him to*

confront Pharaoh, demanding that he let God's people go, but Moses makes excuses and eventually asks God "please send someone else"
- Discuss question 16 on page 41
- Read both paragraphs at bottom of page 43
- Discuss Lesson Summary on page 45

IF TIME REMAINS
- Ask participants if they wish to discuss any questions that were skipped
- Review "Lesson Summary" at the end of the chapter
- Invite participants to discuss any other highlights from the homework they'd like to share

NOTES

~ LUNCH BREAK (30 minutes) ~

CHAPTER THREE: THE CROSSROADS
(taken from pages 183–184)
~ 1 hour ~

OVERVIEW
Abortion is a traumatic experience; however, every woman processes trauma differently. Grief can manifest itself in many ways but no matter where we are, God is willing to meet us there. It is at the Crossroads, where our grief intersects with God's forgiveness, where healing begins.

SHARING OUR STORIES (2–3 min. ea.)
Take turns answering the following questions
- How long ago was the abortion(s)?
- What kind of emotions (if any) did you experience afterwards?
- Did your feelings change over time? If so, how?

HOMEWORK
- Discuss question 1-2 on page 51-53
- Read 2 Timothy 1:9-10 on page 53
- Discuss questions 3-5 on page 54-56
- Review fill-in answers for question 6 on pages 58-59 (consider inviting participants to take turns reading)
- Invite group (including leader/co-leader/helper) to discuss/share their answers to the following questions:

  - Which truth in question 6 do you struggle to believe and why?
  - Which truth in question 6 was most meaningful to you and why?

GOSPEL (pages 60-61)
Acknowledge that someone in the group may have accepted God's offer of salvation for the first time. Invite anyone who made a decision to follow Jesus to share their decision either with the group or, if she prefers, privately with you (or the co-leader) afterwards.

OPTIONAL
Distrubute copies of the poem "Before Me, You." Consider having someone read it out loud. Invite the group to share their thoughts.

REMINDERS
- Present blank Prayer Cards and encourage participants to share their prayer requests (prayer cards to be collected at end of each sessions for leader/co-leader to pray over)
- Advise participants of the importance of carving out time to do the homework each week in order to listen for God's leading. Be mindful that the enemy does not want them to be healed; they are likely to encounter spiritual warfare and distractions along the way
- Attendance: Importance of attending all sessions
- Time: Everyone's time is valuable; importance of arriving on time
- Songs: Invite participants to bring a song to share next time
- Remind participants to complete the homework in Chapter Four for the next session

CLOSING PRAYER
- Closing prayer (pray for participants' prayer requests and for them to sense God's Peace and Presence and as they work through the study)

~

NEXT SESSIONS
For the remaining sessions, continue with Chapter Four: "The Mask" on page 186

NOTES

Additional Forms & Helpful Documents

For your convenience, the following pages include a variety of documents, forms, and poems to enrich your group experience and to help prepare you and the participants for the journey ahead. Keep in mind that not every group uses all forms; choose what works best for you. All forms are available for FREE download at www.shadiahrichi. com. Simply look for the *Worthy of Love* Resources page.

Recommended

- **Group Etiquette Guidelines** (Recommended): This document helps set the tone for the study. It should be distributed and reviewed with all members of the group at the first session.

- **Commitment to Group**: This document is designed to help participants take "ownership" of their commitment to healing. Participants should read, sign, and turn in this form during the first session.

- **Confidentiality Waiver**: Use this form to ensure participants understand the importance of building group trust by committing to keep information shared within the group confidential. Participants should read, sign, and turn in this form during the first session.

- **Sign up/Contact Information** (Recommended): Use this form to collect participants' contact information. Bring to first session.

- **Before Me, You** – a poem (Recommended): This poem is introduced in Session 4. Copies should be provided to all members of the group.

- **A Pre-born Child's Conversation** – a poem (Recommended): This poem is introduced in Session 8. Copies should be provided to all members of the group.

Optional

- **Participant Information Questionnaire**: This form is provided to help the leaders/co-leaders better prepare to serve each participant. Participants should complete the form either prior to or during the first session.
- **Objectives**: This form provides participants with a clear outline of the group's objectives. This form may be helpful for women who arrive at the first session, but who are still considering whether or not to sign up for the study.
- **Support Team Letter**: This document provides participants with a simple way to invite prayer support from friends and family as well as providing friends and family with helpful advice as their loved one journeys through **Worthy of Love**.
- **Evaluation** (Respectfully Requested): Please have each participant as well as leaders/co-leaders complete the evaluation form. This feedback is exceedingly helpful to the ongoing work of the ministry. Forms should be completed at the end of the last session.

Group Etiquette Guidelines

- No Rescuing - Please refrain from advising, analyzing, rescuing, or attempting to 'fix' another member of the group, as this can interrupt or hinder her healing journey. This may be the first time she has been given freedom to grieve; give her space to do so.

- Freedom to Exit – Participants may elect to drop out of the study after attending the first session.

- Commitment – Participants are expected to commit to attend all group sessions and to arrive each week prepared to discuss the homework.

- Respect - This is a non-judgmental Christ-centered group that integrates recovery tools from the study *Worthy of Love*, the Bible, and prayer. Please recognize that participants may have different religious backgrounds.

- Considerate – Please do not interrupt another person while they are speaking (remember "no rescuing"). Be sensitive to the time by not monopolizing the conversation; leave time for each person to share.

- Healthy Environment – No alcohol or other substances that may hinder your ability to fully participate in the group. No cell phones.

- Focus – In order to gain the most from the study, the focus should remain on abortion. At the same time, be mindful that this is not a therapy group. The leaders/co-leaders are volunteers who serve out of their own life experience and do not necessarily have professional training.

- Confidentiality - Due to the sensitive nature of the *Worthy of Love* study, it is important for all participants to keep the information discussed within the study group confidential.

- Arrive on Time - Be considerate of each another's time; please arrive on time.

Commitment to Group

I, _____ (participant) am making

this commitment beginning on _____ (start date)

to _____(end date) with _____

_____ (leaders/co-leaders).

- I commit to attend all sessions except in the case of an emergency.
- I agree to call a group leader if I am unable to attend a meeting due to an emergency.
- I agree to keep in confidence all personal information discussed in the group.
- I agree to do the homework each week and participate fully in the group.
- I agree to share my thoughts, memories, feelings and discoveries with the group.
- I agree to respect and value each member of the group.
- I agree to refrain from discussing the lesson with others until it is discussed with the group.
- I understand that if I arrive under the influence of alcohol or non-prescription drugs, I will be asked to leave and someone will be called to drive me home.
- I agree to abide by the Group Etiquette Guidelines during each session.

I understand and agree to all the above statements and willingly enter into a relationship with the members of this *Worthy of Love* Bible study group.

Note: *Worthy of Love* Bible Studies are offered by grateful volunteers, and do not intend to substitute for any mental health treatment.

Signed _____

Date_____

Confidentiality Waiver

Worthy of Love Bible studies are facilitated by volunteers who have not necessarily been trained in counseling. Consequently, the Bible study and the post-abortion group are not intended as substitutes for professional counseling. Leaders may suggest outside counseling to participants if they see a need.

While the Participant Information Questionnaire is for the group leader/co-leaders use only, all other information discussed within the study group is to be kept completely confidential. At no time are participants to disclose the names of other group members to anyone outside the group. Nor are participants to share part, or all, of another group member's story with anyone outside the group without that member's consent.

There are certain circumstances under which the leaders/co-leaders would be compelled to break confidentiality. For example, if they believe you are at risk for suicide; if they suspect criminal sexual or physical abuse; or if they believe you intend to harm another person.

Due to the sensitive nature of the *Worthy of Love* study, it is important for each participant to be able to trust that what they share with the group will remain confidential. The purpose of this waiver is to confirm that participants understand and agree with this need for confidentiality. Once signed, the group leader will retain this waiver with your personal information.

~

I have read and understand the above. I realize that all information shared during *Worthy of Love* group meetings is strictly confidential.

_____   _____
Participant   Date

_____   _____
Group Leader   Date

Worthy Of Love Study Group

Name	Email Address	Phone Number

Before Me, You

by Shadia Hrichi

Before I entered the womb you prepared for me,
    You knew me.

Before I was born,
        You looked upon me.

Before my first cry,
        You whispered my name.

Before I could walk,
            You carried me.

                Before I turned to you,
                You died for me.

                Before I carried my cross,
    You walked to Calvary.

        Before I whispered your Name,
You cried out for me.

        Before I looked up,
You rose for me.

Before I knew you,
You entered heaven to prepare a place for me.

A Pre-born Child's Conversation With His Heavenly Father
by Delia Baker Hutto March

Father God, when is my mommy going to be here?

Soon, my child, soon.

Can you tell me how long?

There is no measure of time with me, my child.
She is busy right now doing the work I've given her to do.
When all that is done, she'll be here.

Is she going to know me when she gets here?

Yes, she will, my child, I'll let her know.

What does she look like, Father God?

Why, she looks a lot like you, my child. The same color hair,
the same eyes, the same nose,-
you resemble her a lot.

What do you think she's going to do when she sees me?

She will run to you, take you in her arms,
and love you just as any other loving Mother would do.

Father God -why has she never held me in her arms before?

She never had the chance to do so, my child.

Why did she never have the chance, Father God?

I don't remember, my child.

***
*"For I will be merciful to their iniquities, and I will remember their sins no
more."*
(Hebrews 8:12 NASB)

217

Participant Information Questionnaire

The purpose of the Participant Information Questionnaire is twofold. First, having some background information about you will help the group leaders/co-leaders better understand how to support you as you work through *Worthy of Love*. Second, answering these questions will help you begin the important process of thinking back on the abortion(s), perhaps for the first time, as you prepare to move forward through your participation in the study group. The questionnaire is intended for leader/co-leaders use only. No one else will have access to this information without your consent.

You will be invited to share your abortion story with the study group. This is a very important step in the healing process, especially if you have never talked about it with others. As the study gets underway, you will be encouraged to engage in the group discussions as much as possible; to "break the silence." The more you allow yourself to bring details associated with the abortion(s) into the open, the more opportunity there will be for healing.

It may be difficult to recall some details as you go through the questionnaire. That is okay; you are likely to remember more as the study progresses. For now, please answer as completely as possible. Bless you, dear sister, as you begin this journey of hope and healing!

Participant Information Questionnaire

(Confidential information - leader/co-leaders use only)

Name:

Today's Date:

Address:

Email:

Phone:

Date of Birth:

Occupation:

Marital Status: Married__   Separated__   Divorced__   Single__   Widowed__

Abortion History

	Approximate Date of the abortion	Your age at the time of the abortion	Approximately how many weeks pregnant were you?	Abortion type/ procedure
1				
2				
3				
4				

(Use additional paper or the back of this form if you need more space.)

Have you ever sought counseling regarding the abortion(s)? Yes No
If yes, what were the results?

Have you ever been prescribed medication, for example, antidepressants,
for depression or other psychological or emotional symptoms?   Yes   No
If yes, please explain:

Have you ever been or are you currently involved in counseling or support
groups (i.e., AA, drug abuse recovery, grief recovery, sexual or physical
abuse recovery)? Yes   No
If yes, please explain:

How familiar are you with the Bible?
            Not familiar   Somewhat familiar   Very familiar

Thank you for completing the Participant Information Questionnaire.

Objectives of the Worthy of Love Study Group

The primary objective of this study group is to provide you, the participant, with a safe, confidential place to process wounds from past abortion(s). By entering into a community of peers who have experienced similar wounds and stories, you will find encouragement by discovering you are not alone.

A second objective is to help you recognize the destructive beliefs you have held onto, and to replace those beliefs with truths from God's Word. Part of the healing process is to explore and understand sources of destructive beliefs within a safe place, surrounded by others on the same journey.

A third objective is to provide you with meaningful relationships within the study group itself, where you can experience God's unconditional love as well as grace and compassion from others who have walked a similar path.

A fourth objective is to encourage you to take an active role in you healing journey. You are strongly encouraged to take the steps necessary to create space in your life to complete all homework assignments, and to keep a journal (not required, but strongly recommended). You will be expected to attend each session and encouraged to participate in the group discussions.

Support Team Letter

Dear Supporting Friend/Family Member(s):

Your loved one has begun a journey of healing from past abortion by choosing to participate in a post-abortion study group called *Worthy of Love*. As this can be a difficult time, you are encouraged to be sensitive to her needs and, if you are a person of prayer, to pray for your loved one during the course of the study, and in the weeks following its completion.

Here are some ways you can support and encourage her:

- Allow her to share her feelings with you if she expresses a desire to do so. Always let her be the one to initiate the discussion.
- Be a good listener.
- Remind her that healing is a process, and may not happen immediately.
- Be dependable.
- Let her know that you are praying for her.

Thank you for your support!

Evaluation

Your Name: Date:

Your City/State:

1. Did this study meet your expectations? Why or why not?

2. What did you like most about this study?

3. Is there anything you would change about this study?

4. What would you tell someone else who is considering doing this study?

5. May we use your comments to encourage others about the study?
   YES   NO

   If yes, may we include your first name and city/state?   YES   NO

6. Please help spread awareness by rating the book on Amazon.com and Christianbook.com.

Thank you for taking the time to make this Bible Study better for future readers.

Worthy of Love - Leader's Guide
Copyright © 2016 by Beautiful Voice Ministries and
Shadia Hrichi
All rights reserved.
Printed in the U.S.A.

Made in the USA
Columbia, SC
19 November 2020

24915422R00135